TEN MINUTE BUDGET

SPEND LESS - LIVE BETTER

NICK STURGEON

BRIDGEWATER INK

Published by Bridgewater Ink Limited

FOREWORD

I set out to write this book for two main types of reader. Which are you?

The first is for you if you consider yourself to be at the end of your tether financially, stressed about the lack of spare cash each week and worried that your bank account is going into negative, that the payment might be declined when you go to the store for your groceries. I hope that the ideas and suggestions outlined here will give you back control of your spending and provide you with the basic tools needed to get a plan in place that allows you to know where every penny is going. When I started to use the techniques outlined here for myself, several years into my adulting journey, they soon delivered the financial peace of mind that I had been missing.

The second group that I believe can use this book to their betterment are those of you who are actually making ends meet financially, but where you lack a game plan for taking yourself to the next level. Perhaps you pay your bills each month and always have some surplus in your bank that carries you through until the next pay period, but not much other than this. You have debt and are maintaining it or keeping it in place with regular payments, but you are not clearing it off. You have marks against you on your credit file. You feel some pain about your situation but not quite enough for it to hurt you and to stimulate you into real action for change.

There is an incredible opportunity for you to take hold of the information here and accelerate your progress with Clearing Debt and Building Savings. Each of these achievements will give you back the boost of opportunity and excitement you had when you first left college and entered the world of work. A clear Spending Plan will open up the various doors that you have seen closed by your own inaction until now.

I have been in the difficult place of not knowing which bill to pay and how to explain to my other creditors that I can only make a minimum payment. I know the stress of going to the grocery store and guessing the spend amount before my card is offered to the cashier for payment, holding my breath as I wait to see the card approved or declined. I spent years without any savings and being floored when an urgent bill for a car repair or for home heating had to be paid in order for me to keep going, but which meant that my food bill had to be slashed for weeks. Trust that the details, tips and techniques offered here will allow you to step into a better set of circumstances, enabling you to improve your situation.

Read the book with an open mind and give the Ten Minute Budget approach a try by participating in a 30 day challenge. The very least you'll get out of this is a better understanding of your behaviors around money and finding some good solutions to your spending patterns. I believe you will also end the challenge with more money than you expected.

Good luck!

Nick

www.nicksturgeonbooks.com

The basic principles of mastering your money and developing a strong and self-supporting financial habit are really simple. There are two parts to the solution:

First, you commit to looking at your numbers for at least ten minutes every single day.

Second, you must then act on what you observe.

You might be wondering *'Where do I start?'* and that's great. You start with the willingness to look at your financial numbers each day with the intention of seeing them improve because of the actions you take.

For me the breakthrough from being frequently in debt to taking control of my money came in March 2017. The largest source of my income was letting rooms in shared houses to single adults. Most of these people were vulnerable in one way or another, the majority out of work, and in receipt of State aid to cover their housing costs. The government here in the Britain had launched a new scheme for the rent to be covered through a payment method they thought was great. The government thinking was to have one big fund paid out once a month that would give the tenants control of their money and ensure that landlords were getting the rent. But this supposedly fantastic 'all singing - all dancing' new system had so many faults in it that we started to see big gaps in what was due to us as a small landlord compared to what was actually paid. Not just small amounts either. With 57 bedrooms under management and a rent roll of ca $25,000 a month we were seeing random amounts paid. $18,000 one month and then $19,400 the next and then down to $14,750.

As these turnover figures fell and changed, so did my personal income after costs such as tax, local authority bills, building lease charges, utility and cleaning costs. The system was actually in chaos and the government refused to do anything about it, in denial of the mess being created. Month by month I saw our cashflow decimated and over an eighteen-month period I shut down multiple buildings, letting go of more than half the tenants.

Where our tenants had been used to getting their living income on a two weekly basis and had managed OK with this, they were now forced to manage their funds for a whole month instead, something they had never had to do before. They were sticking with old patterns of spending and still using all their cash in the first ten days and then in a state of financial pain for the remaining weeks of the month.

Where we had been able to look at the profitable cashflow from the previous rental income just on a monthly basis, now I was looking at the money every single day and in real fine detail. Over a coffee at the start of each day I hunted for ways to change, cut and adapt my spending. I started to find patterns of money flow, finding new ways to make the rent we did have coming in go further than it had before, cutting costs, shaving expenses and holding onto the cash for as long as possible.

In the space of two months we turned things around and

were able to gain control first of our business funds and then my personal money. I found a happy medium between buildings managed and tenants provided with accommodation meant that we could increase our profits again. At home this translated to more predictable income and the ability to now manage cash flow in way to simultaneously clear debt and build savings accounts. The things I had learned with my work money I implemented at home and the results have been positive and the upturn constant.

Here in Ten Minute Budget I share this approach to developing clear spending habits that create good results. Some of you will love this and accept it in a straightforward way, while others struggle with it. I have been the same way in the past, wanting to complicate something new out of habit rather than accept it for the simple method it can be. This is a practical guide to getting control of your spending and is not filled with theoretical debate.

Money management is an intensely personal subject and there is no one-size-fits-all here. There are various ways for you to take charge and this book intends to provide you with the methods that work and which I have tested for myself, but also through consistent sharing and testing with friends, tenants and work colleagues over these past three years.

For the Ten Minute Budget to have a chance to take hold, and so you can have it work for you, simply commit to the following techniques for the next 30 days. See this as a personal challenge which gives you plenty of time to try for yourself and to gain some of the advantages of controlling your own Spending Plan.

As with all things indie take from the book what you like and what you can make work for yourself and discard other aspects.

I

FACING THE PROBLEM

1

WHAT DO YOU WANT TO CHANGE?

You could well be in a place of real financial struggle. Potentially overwhelmed and hurting at the trouble you face financially, paralyzed to the point of inaction over bills, unable to imagine that things can improve, let alone believing in the potential opportunity for starting a small regular saving plan.

If things are not quite so bleak and desperate as suggested above, you are possibly reading right now because your overall financial position is far from what you want it to be. Perhaps you are carrying several thousand dollars of historic and static debt, are maxed out on a few credit cards from retailers and have no worthwhile savings to speak of.

While imagining you identify with one of these scenarios, I believe that there will be enough practical techniques and suggestions within the pages of this book for you to take action and get real useful benefits.

In making a change from one place to another activity has to happen for you to create something new, different to what you had before. In taking steps to get to a better place with your personal finances you must be willing to adapt and change.

"To know and not to do is not to know".

I forget where in my life I first heard this phrase, perhaps at a weekend self-help workshop back in the day when I was working in London and loved to attend such events regularly, meeting new friends and discovering fresh ideas. It has always stuck with me.

The premise of the message is that if you think you want something, but do nothing to get closer, then it will always be beyond your reach. You can be given an opportunity and fail to act on it. This is like never even having been given the opportunity. You have known for a long time that change has to happen. Don't waste any more time failing to act on your personal finances.

Another quote that has often struck me as remarkable for its strength of message is this one:

"Insanity is doing the same thing over and over again while expecting different results."

It has been attributed to Albert Einstein, to George Bernard Shaw and others, but the actual source is unclear. As a truth about life, it is completely valid.

Are you earning and spending the same amount of money each month, while expecting things to be different this time next year?

Have you been receiving a repeating income, been frustrated by your situation and not tried to reduce your expenses to create a surplus?

Have you incurred the same expenses each month, wanted to create an improved lifestyle, and yet done nothing to boost your income?

You want better results, so you HAVE TO CHANGE YOUR HABITS!

There is no other way around this.

- If your money is not working for you, you must do something different.
- If you are scared of looking at your money, you must do something different.
- If you run out of cash at the end of each month, you must do something different.

You get the picture. Nothing changes until you make the changes yourself. Without a new approach you can have no expectation of an improved situation. If you can accept that you have been kidding yourself this far, now is the time to stop messing about and to knuckle down and start your budget.

So, what do you want? Really. I'm not kidding here, and neither am I waving the magic wand and suggestion affirmations, abundance or a wish list. For sure, such things have their place but just not here.

Right now, this is about you recognizing the mess you are in and taking a daily action for just ten minutes each day to put you in a different mental place around your finance. Your Income, your Spending, your Debt and your Savings. These are the four wheels on your money wagon and you need to give attention to all of them for the journey to become smoother and to get you to a different place from where you are starting out today.

Towards or Away From.

In NLP (neuro linguistic programming) and the ways we can look at changing our thought patterns in order to bring about different results, there is a very useful technique for understanding your motivation and creating change through trialing a fresh approach.

Some of us are motivated by the idea of moving towards the positive images of life. These might feature a nice house in a lovely setting, an image of a beautiful partner whom we adore and are attracted to, scenes of opening our bank statements and seeing good positive account balances, visions of super gorgeous holiday environments and seeing an attractive wardrobe filled with fabulous clothes and shoes. This is the way that a person who has the TOWARDS driver can be motivated through a dream board or a list of positive goals that they consider worthwhile and which they are happy to work towards achieving.

If we are motivated in a different way, by the AWAY FROM drivers, then our perspective is not the same. We will be motivated away from the memory of times when we were unable to eat for lack of available cash for grocery shopping. We will be motivated to avoid the horrible memory of a bailiff knocking at the door and demanding payment of a debt plus charges and the shame we felt at not being able to comply. We will be motivated by not repeating the experience of being in the store when we had a basket filled with the weekly shop and the card was declined at the checkout and there was a queue of people behind us, silently passing judgement.

Having an awareness of these two different ways of being motivated either TOWARDS a positive goal or AWAY FROM negative situations being repeated, this is invaluable as we look at the themes of money and spending. Knowing which of these two most closely represents your own thinking gives you a real strong advantage as we start to look at what it is that you want from developing a budget and a connected spending plan to serve you long term.

Again, what do you want?

If you can improve your financial situation, being able to have a surplus of cash each month and start to save, what will you do with this? Do you have a clear plan in mind of how you will adjust?

- How do you envision things being different?
- What does financial change look like for you?
- What are the bills and regular spends that cause you the greatest stress?
- Can you identify why you feel this way?
- How about building a savings pot to act as a buffer against shock bills or surprise costs?
- What amount do you need to see collected in this separate place from your main bank account?

How will you feel emotionally when - in 30 days or 60 days - you have a better sense of being in control of and fully responsible for the Spending Plan you have crafted for yourself and which is now working for you week after week?

What will 'financially sorted' feel like for you? What will it look like in terms of your home space, the way you organize and manage your financial paperwork and how money exists in your day to day life?

Give some thought to the way your budget will change as you get familiar with all your numbers.

ACTION LEARNING

- How are you personally motivated, Away, From or Towards?
- What overwhelms you most at this moment?
- For how long have you been stuck in repeating the same behavior and expecting different results?
- Why do you think you are ready for change?

2

RECOGNISING YOU HAVE A CHALLENGE

Something is wrong here. You know there is a problem. You just don't want to face up to it right now. The post goes unopened. Every few months your home Wi-Fi gets disconnected because you miss a direct payment from your bank account when funds are less than needed to cover the regular bills. So, you have to call up the collections team and pay over the phone. You are in the supermarket or bookstore and you know you can't buy what you want, so something has to go back on the shelf. It's the start of a new school season and you are dreading the additional cost of new uniforms for your growing children.

What's wrong is you and your money! No one else is to blame. A shame but true. This is your doing, and you can't lay the blame on another. On the positive side this means that getting back in control of your money is a game you can play and win for yourself.

Knowing the numbers are not working

You want to fill the gas tank, but figure you'll just put $40 in and will make do on that level of driving this week. There is a requirement for a new inspection of your air conditioning system at home, but you drag out the call to the engineer until you know you are a week closer to payday. Friends invite you all to come and stay with them for a week at the beach, and you agonize over whether to decline outright or to just say "Yes!" expecting that it will be a tight trip financially with more picnics than meals out at harborside restaurants.

When you are facing this issue of stretching out payments for as long as possible or knowing the numbers can't be met with the money you have, at least you are recognizing the scale of the problem. This is far better than sticking your head in the sand and waiting for the issue to pass by. Here's a free Life Tip for you: the problem will be back again next month and the month after unless you knuckle down and take action to change things. You cannot go on like this!

No more secrets

You and your partner both know there is a problem and yet each continue to spend as if there is no issue. The secrets you keep from each other are not massive to start with. You might creep home with a new magazine or pick up a great looking T-shirt when you are down the mall. He or she brings home some more beautiful crockery and pretends the other items were cracked or chipped. One of you increases the level of your gym membership to include the pool usage and sauna facilities. Perhaps you decide to extend the borrowing facility on your credit card by $500 without sharing this news with your other half.

You are deceiving the person you love, but you are also kidding yourself to the point of real dishonesty. This is not sustainable, and something has to give. That something is your individual or joint lying to yourselves about any of these overspends and additional borrowings. It simply has to stop.

Anxiety and lack of Concentration

You are at a home cooked meal with friends and one of the party asks you a question but you can't remember what they just said to you. In the workplace a colleague requests your thoughts on a new model idea or wants your input during a meeting about how you might do better as a team. You miss the question. Your head is a mess, and your mind is elsewhere. When the mailman knocks on the door you forget this is their regular delivery time and your heart misses a beat in case it is a bill collector.

How about driving down the highway and missing your exit because your thoughts had gone in a different direction, taking you away from being in the moment? This absent minded state and the inability to focus is hugely influenced by your worries and your money thoughts. Instead of keeping them in your head, these need to be discussed between you both as a couple or put down on paper if you need to start to take control of your money and your spending as a singleton. Money is just money. It needs direction from you.

Mentally exhausted

Invited out to events you decline? Leaving social meet-ups early for fear of overspending? Not just because you are not sure you have enough available funds, but also because the idea of trying to be happy and jolly in front of a bunch of friends scares the life out of you. The stress of this is exhausting and you are beginning to lose the plot in several areas of your own personal life and household management.

It's time to put a hold on such damaging behavior and call out the destructive spending behavior for what it is - ignorance, laziness, avoidance and foolishness. You cannot go on borrowing from one account to boost another. Spending on one card to then make a transfer from another that is already very tightly stretched.

It's time to put you first. By this I don't mean that you can have what you want. Instead it is time for you to begin a new focus, one where the attention is on what you need in order to be happy. You have to become fully aware of your money situation each day, pleased with your actions and enjoying the peace of mind which comes from exercising financial self-control. Ten minutes a day is going to bring structure to your finances. Slowly at first and then you will begin to see steady results.

ACTION LEARNING

- How much are you hurting over money matters?
- What lies have you been telling yourself?
- How distracted from life are you because of financial chaos?
- Are you so fed up with being broke, ready to get the budget habit?

3

WHEN YOU CAN'T MEET THE BILLS

A SCARY WAKE-UP CALL CAN COME FROM THE REALIZATION that you have worked a whole month, been paid and still have no more to show for your efforts than a month ago. You are working for a wage and are supposed to be living within your means. This is why it hurts so much to be out of control financially.

Being short of cash, as opposed to being in debt, is a route to feeling upset or even angry about your situation. Yet it doesn't have to be like this always. You can make changes and must make those changes if something different is to happen.

You know the truth of this and have already admitted to yourself things can't continue like this! So, by picking up a book and reading more into the topic you must be keen to get a new set of results. Am I right?

When you have to make a choice between food and getting off the transport network earlier and walking the next section to save costs, or between having the heating on for two hours of an autumn evening versus not having it on at all, then you know you are fairly screwed. As an adult with options and choices you can sit in the hole and feel sorry for yourself or simply start fighting and working to resolve things. I'm going out on a limb here and guessing you are fed up with the status quo and want the change.

Moving out of survival mode is about working at several aspects of your Money Behavior and your Financial Actions simultaneously. You need to be able to see the results which show the difference you are making through such action and the decisions that are now more intentional.

Here are some really quick fixes for the difficult place you are in. Have them here as an easy reference for when you get flustered and worry about being off-track. Each of these will be explored again through the pages of the book. Right now, use these five guide points as a way to place a clear picture in your mind of how you will be getting away from such challenges.

1: Cut your Costs Now

This is the first and most obvious step in the process. Can you take your own food into work, make up a soup or make coffee from a jar instead of buying from a cafe? How about the spare room in your two bed apartment? Is it a luxury you can continue to live with when you might rent it as a long let or try experimenting with the idea of short-term BnB style lets? If you have an annual travel pass for the suburban transport network, what would happen if you kept that for the winter and autumn seasons but cycled and walked the rest of the year? Would a motorbike suit you better than the car?

Are you prone to dropping by the food outlets on the way home from work and buying a take-away which costs five times what you could make the same meal for if you did some DIY food prep.? Have you considered the use of batch cooking and freezing several meals at a time?

Would it really be a big issue of you had a drink with friends twice a month instead of twice a week and what dollar value would you save as money in the bank? Exactly how much did you spend on last year's vacation and what proportion of your credit card debt reflects that you were kidding yourself that you could afford it? Stay home, visit friends, avoid expensive flights, visit local places or simply admit that you cannot afford an expensed holiday this year. If your rent is too high as a proportion of your take-home pay can you look to move somewhere cheaper, just a little walk further from the transport system or from the center of town, simply to reduce your rent by thousands each year? Trim your cell phone plan and use Wi-Fi more than you do currently, cutting your data costs.

2: Boost Your Income

Your next task here is to add to the money coming in from work. You might be able to get extra hours from your employer if you are on an hourly rate of pay. What about an entirely separate new job, something for perhaps an extra ten hours a week? Can you sell some of the things you have around your home? Clothes, music, instruments, unwanted collections of books perhaps?

Can you buy things in bulk or as batches of items and then sell them individually for greater value than the total set? None of these suggestions are to be long-term answers. Right now, you need to bulk up your incoming monies to deal with those debts or borrowings that are keeping you stuck because you are having to allocate some of your savings to debt payment.

3: Find a better Job Role

The less qualified you are the potentially lower your income will be. By looking to further education, more training or a new qualification you give yourself the potential for better earnings and a higher annual income over time.

Is there a role you have wanted but not put in the time or effort to secure the required qualification? Maybe now is as good a time as any to rethink the scope for this. Should you attend a college course, register for some volunteer work in a related category or activity? What can you do in order to increase your hourly rate or overall salary package?

4: Communicate with your Lenders

Pick up the phone and talk to your creditors. If you are repaying $400 a month on a loan but could arrange either a payment break for several months, an interest rate reduction because you have always made your payments or ask for a smaller monthly repayment, what would the benefit of this be to your stress and energy levels?

Can you provide evidence of financial struggle, demonstrate that you are working under a significant debt burden or discuss with them the impact of the debt upon your mental health? Do what it takes to secure a better financial repayment program in order to be better able to manage your overall package of finance. There are some debts you will be repaying in small amounts at a high interest rate where others are currently committing you to large payments on a smaller interest rate. Move things around and find out about a debt swap or settlement of one high interest account by borrowing elsewhere at a better rate of interest.

5: Prioritize Your Own Essential Needs

If you can't meet your rent account and are weak because you are not eating well enough, then the job you have may well go because you fail to turn up on time or fall asleep at work! You absolutely must ensure you are covering your accommodation, utilities, food, clothing and basic transport needs.

You might have to punch your way decisively through some difficult months by cutting your costs everywhere possible. You cannot and must not continue like this. Find a greater sense of balance between your spending needs and getting yourself to a place where your mental and physical health is supported by your financial behavior being on track.

Having a constant watch on your finance allows you more potential for balancing the budget because of the cutting you have done. Moving from being broke to being able to survive each month with a small surplus, this is a great place to get yourself into.

By working to have your costs be just below your income, you have made great strides in closing the month on a positive. Learning to develop a budget - and knowing that this will provide you with different solutions to your spending requirements during varied aspects of the year - is how you get to the place where you can be confident with your money and know that you are becoming financially stronger.

ACTION LEARNING

- Where can you see cost cutting over $100 this week?
- What are you wasting money on by avoiding a budget?
- Why are you scared to start a spending plan?
- What is the cost to you of being out of control?
- How do you want things to look as you change your spending behavior?

II

TALKING ABOUT MONEY

4

CONVERSATION TIME!

Money can be a real taboo, but needs to be dealt with openly as one of the most basic and important elements of a good and healthy relationship. This is money we are talking about. Sex and physical intimacy can be a huge topic for a couple, taking time to build trust and compassion, mutual satisfaction and to develop a real understanding of what you each need from your physical relationship. But money and the discussion of these financial themes between partners can be the greatest of problem topics!

It is easy to feel that we are stepping into an emotional minefield as we broach themes of household finance and shared savings. How about some joint planning for holidays and deciding how to allocate money to things like education, paying the utility bills when they come in? Then there is the covering of school supplies and being able to pay for car maintenance while also wanting to prepare for a well-funded retirement.

You may naturally feel exposed in such discussions. Part of the challenge here is that all of us are raised by family with varying levels of financial competence. In some households the discussion of money is an open book. In others it is a 'dirty' subject, not to be talked about. Some spouses keep money secrets because that is what they were taught as young adults by the example of their own parental role models. We tend to copy our parents based on the idea that they know what is best for us. Years later we discover, often in shock, that in some areas we could have been given much more insight. As adults we are free to select a new behavior that will work for us.

We can find it easy to mention in passing to a friend during a walk or to a work colleague over a canteen lunch that we might be *a bit short this month*" or that "*I'm holding my breath financially until payday*". These sorts of comments are easily made, and yet rarely go into the real frightening truth of the situation. If you are in a couple, then you need to have 'the talk' together and the sooner the better.

I have written elsewhere about the topic of debt in my book 'Climbing Out of Debt'. In that title I deal as constructively as I can about the strategies for recognizing the debt burden and then working your way systematically through these debts, and doing so in such a way that you are no longer drowning under the pressure of them.

Talking about consciously managing your money habits, of the skills and repeated approach - this is what the Ten Minute Budget is all about - can be the hardest discussion between two people who love each other in every other aspect of their relationship, and yet cannot find the language, the space, the communication skills or the ability to sit down and say: "*I think we are messing up. Can we work together and do something that will change out finances for the better?*" Putting it this way makes it sound far tidier and more polite than some of the early conversations I had about money with my better half.

In the past I've had some real big arguments about

finance with a former partner. Not surprising really, given that I was behaving like I could have anything I wanted and spending sometimes as though we had an unlimited bank balance. Tensions are raised along with voices. One of us might feel OK talking about detailed numbers while the other is terrified even by the vaguest suggestion of personal financial responsibility. The private discussion about money as adults is not really something which childhood prepares us for. That said, there is such opportunity now for you to find a way to manage and handle such a conversation.

Being able to communicate well together about money and how you allocate and then spend it together as a couple and as a united household, this is an incredibly valuable skill set to acquire. It requires work, patience and practice to get good at it, just like any worthwhile aspect of a relationship. To respect and listen to your partner in this will sometimes be very difficult. They rightly have an opinion of their own. Just like you they need to be able to safely express this. Talking together about money can be a scary process to begin with, and you will do well to protect the time and space in which you let this discussion of Household money and Personal finance happen.

It doesn't happen quickly, but it will start to become real once the two of you can say to one another - and preferable kindly - *"Enough is enough. Let's talk about money together."*

Some tips to help

Agree a time together when you will sit down to talk about finance.

Avoid a *'we have to do this right now'* approach and instead agree a date. Take the conversation away from the home if you want to. Go to a coffee shop, or to a picnic table in a local park. Being away from the home environment can make it just a little bit easier for you to step out from patterns of usual behavior.

Set a maximum time for the first discussion. This might just be 30 minutes. For many of us this limiting of the first conversation means we can face it and know that there is an end to the discussion of something that can be as worrying as talking about money. When you reach the preset time limit and feel able to talk some more, then go ahead.

Make some notes and bring these with you into the discussion space. Write down what you would like to talk about, the item that is concerning you, how you might now like to approach a spending element in a different way than before or how you feel that between you a revised budget limit can be applied to some of your existing household spends.

Try these easy starters to look at ideas and assumptions that you have been working with:

- Where do your own money and budgeting assumptions come from?
- Who do you think gave you some of the learned personal habits you have around cash and credit?
- What money lessons did you receive from your parents?
- What money discussions do you remember seeing or overhearing between your parents?
- How did those observations make you feel?

Remember that you love this person. In any joint discussion you are both equal. There is no 'Right and Wrong'. Instead there are behaviors around money and spending patterns that are working or not working. This is not personal. Money is not personal. Money goes where you direct it to go.

After the first conversation about your household budget, talk together about how you each felt it went. Stay gentle.

This is not about criticism or disagreement and instead is about learning to talk about money. This is going to take courage, commitment and regular time set-aside just for this theme. The person you are discussing money with is your partner in life and as such this is a conversation that will evolve over time as you grow together. Money worries, perspectives, attitudes and responsibilities around respecting your partner's viewpoint on these are as much a part of intimacy within your relationship as is anything else that is special, important and private to you both.

Consider the trust that comes from knowing that your partner seeks to protect you against financial fear and work with you to secure outcomes around household finance which will see you working closely together and winning as a couple.

Establish a time for another discussion in one week. Put the time in the diary and make it a 'money-date'. It is an intimate discussion about something intensely personal to the two of you.

ACTION LEARNING

- How soon can you book to have 'the talk?'
- What might go on your agenda for the budget conversation?
- Identify your overspending and put a number on it.
- Look at practical routes to saving the money you can create from sensible cost cutting.

5

BE IN THIS TOGETHER

Talk about money together? You can't be serious!

Actually, I am very serious about this. If you are in a relationship, then you absolutely must get your joint thinking straight about this topic. Your money is your shared money. Do you both work and put your income into a joint account? If not, why not? Is one of you not earning while the other holds down a job. How do you work together to establish your budget and spending plan?

You have shared visions, so let your money work in the same way, being something that allows the two of you to move closer to those same goals. By all means have an individual pot or fund for each of you in order to have little treats and to build-up to the point of getting something special that you have saved for and looked forward to having. But right now, in terms of your banking have one account that combines your household income. It's that simple!

Have a regular household meeting to discuss finance. Set this aside as a half hour for each week. Establish a simple agenda, not because you need to manage the time tightly, but just so that you can discuss the things you want to without forgetting or missing some aspects of your spending for this week or for the financial planning of the month ahead.

Set down some rules for what a household money meeting might look like or feel like. It could be at your kitchen table on a Sunday evening, or the local indie coffee shop on a Saturday morning. Give it a time limit and finish on time. Don't be putting yourselves under any pressure that you cannot cope with. The first few times you sit down together to discuss money, to start chatting about themes or topics you might potentially be nervous about, take care to be gentle on yourselves. This is not a race, and you will be the winners by getting this right between you.

Working together on your money, you are giving yourselves the opportunity to better your relationship in the process. Enjoy setting the time aside for these discussions.

6

YOUR LIFE, YOUR MONEY

IF YOU ARE SINGLE AND WORKING ON YOUR MONEY management and budgeting skills, you don't have to do this entirely alone. For sure, you get to deal with it from the perspective of your own plans and goals. That is not the same as meaning you have to struggle with the process on your own.

As a single person what you earn is yours and yours alone. You get to keep everything that you bring home financially after tax and contributions have been paid. In theory at least, all is good, and you can do what you want with your money. Except that this is a book intended for those who are deep within the struggle to make ends meet, to balance the budget, to have money left over at the end of the month rather than the other way around!

You can really benefit from speaking with a friend as a sounding board to where your money is right now versus what you want the situation to look like in a few months. There will be at least one or two friends who you know you can sit down with and talk through the situation together. To open up to someone about money is as hard as any intimate subject and you will want to carefully select who it is that you sit down with.

It doesn't need to be a family member before a work colleague or a social friend ahead of a person you know within a neighborhood project. But it absolutely does have to be someone you can trust to keep the detail of your discussions private. It might need to be a person whose own financial behaviors you consider as ones you admire. Once you have chosen a person to approach you will find it helpful to be able to explain what you need from them as part of their supporting you.

You are looking for a person who will listen as you talk about your situation and who will be respectful of the fact that you are discussing very personal topics. You are seeking a person to be an accountability partner for you, whom you can open up to and then share regular updates with about the state of your finances. Explain to them what you think will be needed, how often you might need to meet in person or speak via online technology to discuss bank statements, earnings, tracked expenditure, money owed and savings goals.

Approach one of your friends and ask them if they are willing to be a trusted partner in the process of helping yourself get back on track financially. You cannot borrow from this person. You cannot pay them for their support. Their role is to be there for you, to listen, not to judge, and to give you suggestions when they feel you are veering away from a support agreement.

Enjoy taking them out for coffee and a cake to a place you really like. Share your numbers with them while they do the same with you. Look through bank statements, payroll info, the balance of your savings accounts and the detail of what your budget goals are. Write down some goals for the week and the month. Look at what you will spend on the categories of Accommodation, Transport, Clothing, Savings, Food and Holiday funding. If you have Debt then include this as an additional category, bringing the account information and owed balances to the same regular discussions. Make sure to also look at what you might do with some of your personal goals from the savings pots that you set aside and to fund personal development and more financial education.

You can gain such value from the process of working with someone as your own accountability partner, supporting each other in moving closer to the goals you select as meaningful to yourself.

ACTION LEARNING

- Who can you approach to be an accountability partner?
- What support do you need from them for you to feel safe in this discussion of your numbers?
- Have you identified the money issue you want to tackle first?
- If debt is involved be sure to know the amounts and interest rates.

III

COUNTING THE CASH

7

WHERE DOES IT ALL GO?

TRACK EVERY PENNY.

Being clear about your money - and then taking action for change - is how you will become free of debt. Clarity over your finances, one day at a time, is where you start with this process and stop your poor spending habits.

Today I want you to track every penny, cent or dime that passes through your hands. It won't necessarily be an easy exercise but will be a simple one. The reason that you need to do this is so that you know beyond any doubt where your money is and what the numbers look like. It's very common for a person a financial mess to not know the detail of the money that is passing through their hands at all. To not even have a clue! I call this Money Blindness, with the vision for any detail completely missing.

Try this for yourself. I'm going to assume that you know the cost of your rent or your mortgage payment to the nearest dollar? If you don't then we have a real problem!

But how about the amount you spend at coffee shops in a month? What about the cost of groceries on that Tuesday evening shop after work three weeks ago? How much did you spend last month on TV and Internet channels and magazine subscriptions? What did it cost you on this most recent month's mobile phone bill? Do you really know? How much did you spend on car maintenance, servicing and parts these past twelve months? Scary questions? Am I getting too deep with the request for information?

Do I Have To?

No. Is it OK for you to lurch from one unexpected expense to another and with no real sense of where you will get the money from to cover these? How about fear, embarrassment, shame, nervousness, guilt and distress? Would letting go of these emotional states be something that you would accept willingly in exchange for adopting and learning a couple of really simple approaches to dealing with your money? I do hope so. All it takes is the daily commitment of around ten minutes to your household budget.

Just for today carry a small notepad or a folded sheet of paper with you and write down exactly what you spend money on. To the exact penny.

Today my own notes look like this so far:

Car fuel	£30.00
Cappuccino	£ 3.80
Grapes	£ 2.00
Pastries	£ 1.40
Sandwich	£ 3.50
Fruit	£ 1.20
Toiletries	£ 4.97
Laundry	£10.00
Total	£56.87

It's only mid-afternoon right now and I would expect to add some entries later for a meal out. Maybe some stationery for the office, possibly stamps at the Post Office. The more you log the full detail of your expenditure the less random and more conscious your spending pattern becomes.

Why keep a Spending Record?

We get money in and we let it out. We rarely track it, analyze trends, look for patterns, think about the movement, or consider much about it. But by the end of a first full day of monitoring this, your notepad will show you where you are spending the money.

Here's the other reason for keeping this Spending Record. It closes the gap between you and your money precisely because you are asking for a receipt for everything, and because you write down the cost of that latte before you actually take the first sip from the cup. If you enjoy it, you will appreciate what it cost you. If you have to write down the cost and then consider that you could have spent the money on something else for greater satisfaction or sense of value then the process of recording the spending has helped you to think more acutely about how you are using your money. Double bonus!

You have to take out your pen and note the cost of the newspaper or magazine before you turn the pages. You must write down the cost of the tank of fuel before you turn the key in the ignition to drive off. In each transaction you are noting the cost. At the close of the day simply do your ten minute tally of the numbers and see where you chose to spend money today.

What do you see on the paper outside of the actual numbers? You get to identify very clearly the choices that you are making over what you want to spend your money on. It's right there in front of you. How do you feel about what you see? Notice your reaction to some of the things that you have spent your cash on.

So here's a potential list from your spending day:

Cash	4	Coffee
Card	27	Stationery shop
Card	32	Bag of Groceries
Card	40	Clothing Item
Cash	3	Postage Stamps
Cash	4	Birthday Card
Card	40	Fuel from Garage
Cash	6	Sandwich and soft drink
Cash	5	Cleaning products
Cash	2	Chocolate bar
Cash	4	Another Coffee!
Card	19	Takeaway Food Order
Card	8	Pack of Beer
	194	

Next Steps after your Daily Record.

Now you translate this into a whole week with a summary of the previous 7 days of notes that you have made. Are there any items on the summary that might cause you to feel awkward or anxious about your spending behavior? This exercise is only for you. No-one else is looking over your shoulder at this stage. This is your own very personal Spending Record. So if you see stuff on the lists that you think you could actually do without or perhaps buy less of, again it's completely fine to use this as a good reason to shift the direction of some of your spending. You cannot change a situation from a position of ignorance of the truth. Equally you cannot expect to change your spending patterns until you know what they are.

The first month I ever did the Spending Record exercise the thing that really upset me was how much I was spending on a can of beer here, a couple of bars of chocolate there, some fast food here, etc. In the course of a given week I could now see that I was choosing to hand over my hard-earned money for things that were my attempt to drown out my sadness and frustration about my situation. I was using a sugar rush to mask my upset about the way my life was. A few tins of beer each night was my attempt to paint over my feelings of not living the life that I thought I should be enjoying. But £4 a night on beer here in England meant £1,460 (this is almost $1,900) would have no chance to reach my savings account that year! I realized that the same £1,460 could do much better things if directed elsewhere.

Instead of looking after myself, treating myself to the relaxation of cooking a healthy meal after work, I was buying a container of fast food and numbing myself to the pain of unhappiness. It was glaringly obvious to me that I was out of control. I was neglecting to make time for the pleasure of preparing my own food, and then enjoying a home cooked meal. By maintaining the Spending Record over the course of a day, then a week and across a whole month it served as a wakeup call. For this reason, I regard the Spending Record as a very powerful habit for you to practice in order to give you the insight into your use of money. Take what you learn from doing it as a motivator to get yourself into a good place about getting free of your debt.

So, do it now. Do it today. Understand that your Spending Record informs your Budget.

Tools to Help.

As a young man in my first full-time job I used the pages of a Filofax which came with lots of handily designed sheets to track money in and out. Nowadays, all types of journals and day planners exist to support you in monitoring to tracking your spending. Many of these can be bought cheaply at supermarkets as well as stationery stores, and the journal will often have a pocket in the back for you to keep tickets and receipts. Online software and apps for your phone make the ability to see pictures of your spending very easy indeed. You can just as easily insert spending items into your phone app and build up the spending pattern during the day, seeing it on a large screen when you get back to your laptop or PC. If you are visually motivated these tools will be a real help. If you are tactile in your approach, then pen and paper will be what works for you. The key thing is to find a process that is easy for you because you enjoy it. If it's complicated, you won't be giving yourself any incentive.

A pocket notebook that is easy to fit in your coat or an envelope, either of them can fulfil the role of a place to store your receipts. There is no need for you to spend any real money to capture the record of where you spend and what you buy with your money. The key is to make sure every expenditure gets logged somehow.

If you buy with a debit card at the shop counter or the service station you will naturally be given a receipt. With simple cash transactions at the hardware store or in the green grocer shop you will either have to ask for a receipt or finish the purchase, reach for your notebook and write down what you just bought and the cost of it. Just ten minutes a day to log your spending and educate yourself to the truth of where your money has been disappearing.

If you're reading this at lunchtime you can still start to log your spending until you go to bed tonight. Tomorrow you can do a full day of recording the way that money is going through your hands.

Simple Rules.

1. Record each expenditure. Don't miss one.
2. Write down the detail as soon as you can after spending the money
3. Log the exact amount, to the actual penny.

It's really simple to do this. From now on, you'll not be putting $50 in your pocket at the start of the day and then be wondering at night why you have just $7.37 left over in change. You will know where the money went and what you spent it on. Your left over cash and receipts, plus your own simple notes, will show you where the other $42.63 went during the day!

Maintaining the daily record and learning from the pattern of your spending in this way, puts you back in control, not just of your money but of your life. From knowing the numbers behind your spending, you then become conscious of your choices over what you buy. Only once you are fully aware of this can you start to make better informed decisions about saving, investing and further spending.

The Weekly Record.

This is just a summary of all the information that you give yourself from the previous seven days. Keep it simple and make sure the numbers are accurate. So, run a week at the start of a month in the 1st day and include the 7th day. Start the next week on the 8th and include the 14th. Take you individual single day records and add them up to calculate the week.

If there are two of you in this exercise, then you need to each keep a record of your own and share them at the end of the week. It will be fascinating to compare notes and observations that you make as this week ends. Let's not even get into the issue of you perhaps having different incomes. We might be brave enough to approach this in another chapter! For now, you each keep your own daily, weekly and monthly records. Your combined goal once you've done this is to take a good look at the money and where you are spending it.

Monitor your Paperwork.

Your notebook or journal might not contain the whole truth. Because you have a bank account and may be running regular monthly payments or standing payment arrangements from it, there will be payments from the account that also need to be noted and included within your records. It's easy to overlook the passive payments in the background such as these, so check your bank account for the weekly record and ensure you have accounted for these when getting the full picture on your numbers.

Assuming you have a full and accurate record of where the money goes, you can divide the expenditure by 100 to create a percentage view of where you have spent your hard earned cash.

Match the percentages against the categories that you can see within your spending behavior. Categories might be as general as House, Car, Clothing, School Fees, Food, Social and Holidays.

These would then break down more specifically to:

House

Rent / Mortgage, Insurance, Gas, Electric, Wi-Fi, Cell Phone, Water, Repairs, Laundry, Appliances inc. TV, Local Taxes.

Car

Road tax, Insurance, Fuel, Valeting, Tires, Accessories, Maintenance.

Clothing

Replacing worn clothing, Seasonal clothes, Boots, Shoes, Repairs.

School

Meals, Fees, School Travel, Textbooks, Educational Trips, Club Memberships.

Food

Home, Work, Travelling Food, Gym Supplements.

Social

Dinners Out, Birthdays, Drinks, Club Memberships, Gym Fees, Hobby materials, Coffee Shops, Bars.

Holidays

Savings account for holidays, Food, Travel costs including air tickets and car hire.

If by this point you have begun the process of collecting the information on your daily and weekly spending, you will have made real effort to do this. Rest assured that this is a big part of the battle that is getting in control of your money. Now that you know where you have been spending you can confidently go forward, looking at why you spend where you do, and deciding on how you might want to change current spending priorities for some that potentially support you better.

ACTION LEARNING

- Decide how you will track every spend.
- Your notebook will show you where the money is going.
- Review your spending every day.
- Your new mottos is "Every dollar gets logged."
- Check your monthly bank statements to include automated payments.

8

BUDGET ALLOCATION

WHERE DO I PLACE MY MONEY?

In establishing good use of your money there are some approaches you might want to hear about and consider their application in your own situation.

Pareto and the 80 / 20 Rule

The much talked of 80/20 Rule draws on the Pareto principle (look it up and learn more) that 80% of what you do is largely ineffective and that 20% of your actions might create 80% of the important results. The history of this principle is an old one and where it can be applied to Budgeting and your Personal Finance, you need to be careful. If 20% of your income went to Savings things would be good, but this leaves 80% almost 'flying in the breeze' and undefined. To say that 80% of your income should simply be labelled as being 'for any other costs' is too vague to be helpful.

If the 80/20 Rule is at one end of the spectrum, then the creation of spreadsheets that track every dollar of income and spend might be seen as too detailed. Not for some, I have to say and certainly there have been times when I have managed my income and costs for several months always down to the nearest dollar in order to attempt to track each amount.

Broad Brush approach 50 / 30 / 20

You want to create a Spending Plan, but perhaps don't want to make an intricately detailed line-item budget or budgeting worksheet. Instead, you just want a budget that represents a "broad overview." Further away from the spreadsheet is the 50/30/20 budget where 50% is living costs, 30% goes to accommodation and 20% to savings (including debt reduction).

Five Element Approach

If you want an approach with potentially more specific direction then this might well be it. I have tried both of the previous 80 / 20 and then the 50 / 30 / 20 percent approach, each for three months and more before deciding not to continue with them. I found them a little too vague for me, and noticed I was not saving strongly because it was not an aspect dealt with in any detailed way.

The broader approach of the Five Category approach (I am calling it this for the sake of simplicity, but it goes by a variety of names and labels), works well for many people because it gives you five places to focus on with your use of money. These are approximate percentage allocations of after tax or take-home income, to be directed to the five main categories that you are going to be working with each month.

35%	Housing / Accommodation
15%	Transport
25%	General Living
10%	Savings
15%	Debt Reduction

With this general approach you get some more categories than the other two models, can see the balance or ratio between each of them to one another, and can see how you might have some useful flex between these five suggested categories for your spending. (Notice that this model gives you a focus to building savings from every single income receipt).

Here we are looking at your **Housing / Accommodation** spend being up to 35% of income (and this includes rent or mortgage, utilities, household maintenance and repair, property or council tax, water charges, insurance and furnishing). On consideration you feel you can manage these at lower balance of ca 30%, then of course you are free to use that remaining 5% somewhere else to suit your needs as a household. You could put it into **General Living** (food, eating out, life insurance, school costs, clothes, entertainment, holiday budget) where until now you have been allocating 25% of your income to be used.

Or you are happy with **General Living** costs being 25% and you instead move that flexible 5% into **Transport** (car finance, vehicle insurance, maintenance, public transport like subway, train, tram and bus) then you could use this extra to get your car finance paid down faster.

Savings as a category within your budget should be 10% or more of received income. (You can start with 10% and split this amount between a longer-term retirement focussed account and the creation of first one and then several small cash balance accounts. Such accounts are where you steadily build up some cash to protect you against the sort of $1,000 or $2,000 challenges or emergencies which crop up from time and simply need you to be able to throw a bag of money at them without getting worried about other expenditure being thrown off course. If you have no such money set aside then even a small sudden bill can have the effect of knocking you sideways.

The function of such accounts is to give you a breathing space or a protective defence against financial incidents. (You will have perhaps heard of these as being called Emergency

Funds by some people and Sinking Funds by others). If your car needs a repair that is standard maintenance - perhaps as part of the annual service - you could be presented with a $400 bill. While you were not exactly expecting this precise figure it is a part of car ownership and you need to settle the bill. If you don't have the $400 spare cash to hand, rather than borrow the money on your credit card, you simply draw down $400 from a Short-term Savings Fund / Emergency Fund type of account and pay with confidence.

With the remaining balance of your allocated budget being 15% of the 100% you get to place this against the clearing of **Debt** commitments such as loans due, credit card balances that are stuck and which remain month after month, personal loans and perhaps some student finance.

As before, you get total choice on where you might move a spare 5% between one category where it is not needed and to instead throw it at something which needs more attention and focus. To put the surplus against either Debt reduction or the boosting of Savings is going to be a good thing so long as you have protected and covered the requirements of the other three categories of Housing / Accommodation, Transport and General Living.

Grasp these five categories quickly and have them in your mind as you receive and then allocate or distribute your income. Regardless of whether you earn and are paid weekly or monthly, it is vital to understand your personal spending plan and to be making progress in the areas of Debt and Savings. With the three main categories being well covered - and absorbing 75% of your spending - you can create the headspace to make good progress on the other two 'pots' of money.

Perspective is Everything

Purists from one camp or another in the debt free community might say you have to clear debt in total before you put anything into savings. I don't hold that view as I believe that you need savings to get you though the inevitable challenges that can come along from time to time and which will derail you financially if you have no cash set aside. (I have been broke with savings available and then in a desperate mess without the protection of having built up a small cash safety net. I know which one was the more practical approach to have adopted). You have to make your own mind up on these things and pick the standards that work for you and your thinking.

Stepping back to look at your budget and at your patterns of spending , consider the Five Category approach. The emotional power of establishing where you see yourself spending money and beginning to ring fence such location is enormous. As you compile your household spending record through the use of a notebook or via an app on your phone you will see very obvious opportunities to cut costs, reduce spending and gain the level of clarity that enables you to have practical and firm control of your budget.

Winner's Gain - The real advantage of this flexible percentage approach is that once you have cleared each debt you have a choice to make over whether you throw all the money or some of the available and freed up resource to more clearing of debt. It might be the case that you consider you can bolster your retirement fund while making steady progress on debts that are far more under control than they appeared to have been a year before when things were more frightening to you.

ACTION LEARNING

- Have you identified your Essential Needs spending?

- Do you know and understand the percentage for each category?
- Where might you cut costs and provide a surplus within each category?
- In which area of spending have you been the laziest?

9

THE 'FORGOTTEN' SEVEN

WHEN YOU SIT DOWN TO CONSTRUCT A BUDGET YOU CAN WORK with, a very common mistake is to leave several categories out of the overall calculations. Most obvious is the assumption that you start with the cost of groceries, add cost of your household utility bills, add some more for a holiday and months later wonder why you have no money left and are still running some debts.

There are seven categories of spending which we can often leave out of our budget planning. Include these and allow for them early on and you are more likely to have a better feeling of control over your spending.

1. Retirement
2. Eating Out
3. Gifts
4. Entertainment
5. Daily Treats
6. Clothing
7. Annual Bills

Retirement

This is not a popular topic when you think it is tough enough to survive right now that you are having to remind yourself to budget every dollar you have. I know that! This is why I have placed it first here in this list of things we can forget to account for.

Your employer might be putting something into a pension plan but that doesn't not mean it will be enough for you to have a comfortable retirement. Just because you are managing - just about - right now on a full time income, what gives you to think that this will be any less difficult when you have free time every day but no salary and the costs are still there for you? Get real about this and allow for money to go into a long term savings account. I am labelling it here as being specifically for Retirement as distinct from the savings accounts mentioned earlier for unexpected expenses. This money is not for anything else.

Eating Out

You will know your most common spend as weekly food shopping. But what about the drinks with a friend after work on a Friday night, the takeaway on a Saturday or the impulse meals purchased in a restaurant during a long drive? We tend not to think about these but the cost of them - if you take the effort to track them - adds up to significant total figures.

In a personal example, I recently took my youngest son back down to university in preparation for the new term. We stopped for coffee and a sandwich on the journey down, spending the equivalent of $20. When we were in Oxford we went to a gorgeous canal-side pub on the first night. We sat outside and spent $80 on food and drink. The next day we visited my eldest son in his neighboring town and the three of us enjoyed another tasty meal at a good restaurant for $120. So, in the space of two days I dropped $220 on food and refreshment that was not my normal food spend. By comparison, in a typical week I stock up on regular items for my kitchen cupboards and budget ca $60 for this. So, in this week with some driving and other visits I added $220 extra, boosting my food related spend massively.

What about yourself and the meals you eat away from home? For example, what do you spend on a work lunch? You might be fortunate and be in a large company that has an in-house cafe or restaurant, or you might nip out during the lunch time and buy a drink and a sandwich at a local shop. Either way there is a daily cost to all of this. If you spend even $15 a day on a midday snack, then you need to account for the $75 you are adding to your costs for those five days of snacking in your work week. I don't wish to scare you but in 48 working weeks you are shelling out $3,600 on lunchtime snacks at $15 per day. What else might you be able to do with such funds and having them create more meaningful and longer lasting results?

When you are drafting your first spending plan, make sure to allow for the extra cost of Eating Out. Make it a category you include within the budget.

Gifts

These are needed at various times across the calendar. A nephew does well at school. Your aunt achieves a community award. Some friends get married. Festivals and religious holidays mean present expenditure. Family members have birthdays and presents are given.

You don't need to be thrown off balance by these so long as you think about the likelihood of such costs during the year. Set something aside for what might seem like a reasonable number of presents and maintain this money in an account for the purpose or in an envelope that suits you better. Be realistic with the numbers and true to yourself. This means being detailed while also gifting only what you can really afford.

Steer clear of the social pressure that we can all imagine. Place only your own household financial situation at the heart of your budget decisions. Do not gift or give money to a cause or charity when you are in financial need yourself! Don't increase your debt to give a gift. Often a card and a special message can be enough whether within or outside of your immediate family.

Entertainment and Relaxation

When you are busy and engaging well with life you are happy. So make sure that you allow for the cost of a night out with friends, a regular date night with your partner, for the cost of taking the family out for a cinema evening or a session at the swimming pool and a meal after. When I was at my poorest it was so easy to say a firm 'No' to entertainment costs, yet the knock-on effect of this can be a loss of morale, resentment at the actual budget process and then an unwillingness to stay with the spending plan. Isolation can cause mental health issues and there is a measurable positive benefit to have and enjoy some social activity, but never at the price that your budget cannot afford or justify.

If you find yourself resenting the management of your spending plan or the monitoring of your Ten Minute Budget, let me suggest that you lost sight of your reason WHY. You want to be in control of your personal finance, to have the ability to know what you can do with your money and to enjoy the benefits of this knowledge.

Entertainment and leisure can involve spending some of your budget on activities you enjoy, that lift your spirit and boost your mood. All of these are good for your well-being. There is a mass of free activities you can do for yourself and with your household that cost nothing. Please don't lose sight of the fact that you can entertain, amuse and educate yourself without any spending.

Visit a city or country park. Walk around your neighborhood. Spend a weekend hour in a municipal art gallery. Invite friends over for a potluck lunch. Enjoy a book-swap with neighbors. Host an evening of board games. Skype or Zoom with a relative or friend who lives at distance. Start a journal. Subscribe to half a dozen new blogs and podcasts about the stuff that fascinates you. Clean up that bike, add some sidebags and get outside on an urban or countryside exploration trip.

Protecting and nurturing your mental and emotional condition is so important. Don't for a moment be fooled into thinking that this is a function of your wallet, paycheck or income status. Make time to do the things you love and recognize the health benefits of putting your happiness and wellness above your need to have your personal finance numbers instantly sorted. You can track your money and live within your budget while still actively making time to do many of the things you enjoy.

You are committed to getting a handle on your money. Don't stop looking after yourself at the same time as you steadily recover your budget. Allocation a portion of your funds to your entertainment and relaxation. Never lose sight of the importance that your own happiness and positive mental healthheath plays in getting you through these tough times.

Remember the powerful phrase that Robert Schuller was famous for saying

"Tough times never last, but tough people always do."

Look after yourself in all of this.

Daily Treats

This could be the coffee on the way to work, the chocolate in a slow afternoon, or the book that you see in the bookstore and just have to buy to lift your spirits on a rainy afternoon in town. Perhaps you buy an extra four pack or case of canned drinks once a month during your grocery shop? This might be considered a food shop item but if you do it to lift your spirits or boost your mood then it is a purchase driven by your need for a treat. Such items as these are frequently relatively low in cost, perhaps $5 to $10 dollars each, but two of these a week can easily add up to $1,000 and more in the year.

I'm not suggesting you cannot have such little treats, but what can you achieve with the redirection of that same $1,000 to a different use? Just apply some thinking to your impulse spending and become more conscious of their cost by allowing for them within the numbers you include in your budget.

Clothing

If you are a clothing diva then this category can completely wreck your budget, simply because you think you have to have such an item when it is launched in the stores. Maybe you think there is a link between your popularity and what you wear? Get over this one quickly and realize that your actual friends like you for who you are and not for your wardrobe attachment! Thousands of dollars on clothes hanging in your wardrobe will do nothing to clear debts and boost savings.

Forgive me if you think that was an extreme example. But do watch out for the temptation to get a new coat each season or a different bag, rucksack, laptop carry case etc. just because you have had one for a year already. Include the need for some new shoes, a coat, fresh underwear, adequate winter clothing. Where you can, keep your new wardrobe costs as low as possible while you are managing money more tightly for better long term results and intentions. Include or allocate some spend each month for clothing and footwear even though you might actually only shop for such items a couple of times in the year. Have some cash set aside for when the opportunity presents itself.

Annual Bills

Another easy way to be tripped up with bills is to forget those that can come just once or perhaps twice a year. These can include home taxes or area taxes (council tax as it is called in my country). You can pay monthly or annually, but remember to account for these annual bills so that you are not taken by surprise. On your vehicle insurance you can save money by paying once per year instead of a more expensive route via monthly payment. Keep your eye out for such variations in cost and - as you make progress with your other more regular bills - consider the cost advantages of switching just some of your costs to annual payment.

ACTION LEARNING

- Which of the Forgotten Seven is your frequent weakness?
- How do you most frequently overspend?
- Why are you choosing to live beyond your financial means?
- What can you do this week to gain more control of your budget?
- By cutting down on Daily Treats how much can you save for something you really want?

10

USING THE ENVELOPE SYSTEM

This can work for some people and is the tightest way to manage things. Very little flexibility and requires a lot of self-discipline. Then again, why would I want to give out the message that this should be easy, fun and that there is nothing to worry about. That would be irresponsible of me. I am going to be strict with you, but nowhere near as tough as you will need to be with yourself.

This is your money and your financial life we are talking about. Money stress can damage or break relationships. It can lose you a job or lead to distraction at work when you need to be on the ball.

My parents had a green Money Tin at home when they were first married. The tin has various slots in the lid for money to be allocated in different themes of weekly spending: Rent, Food, Coal, Bus, Clothes, Education, Holiday. Those were the seven things neatly written by hand on each label on the lid. I still have the tin today and I love what it represents. It symbolizes the journey that this young couple embarked on together in their tiny rented flat long before myself and my siblings were born.

For me starting to get my budget right happened quickly because I adopted the concept of allocating money to specific categories, just as Mum and Dad had done. Money tins seem to have been successfully replaced by a popular method that works well for many people these days and which is called The Envelope System.

Using this approach, you start by working out where your money goes over the week. To reach that decision you will need to track what you spend for the next seven days.

Start with a pen and paper and consider where you have already spent money today and where you think other expenditure will happen across the rest of this week. Sketch out the week and where you think you will have costs.

Your initial categories could be broad like Accommodation, Transport, Clothing, Groceries, Technology, Travel. This is fine and you can refine as you track.

Next week you might have identified: Food at home, food and coffee on commute, meals at work. Public transport or vehicle maintenance, fuel, car insurance, breakdown cover, vehicle finance. Clothing. Utility bills, Wi-Fi, film platform or streaming services, mobile contracts. Finance on technology. Pension contributions in addition to employer contributions. Money to savings. Cost of annual holidays.

Consider which of your spending categories you will move to Cash.

Notice that not all of the categories you have started to identify as you track your spending will be for Cash money. You will have regular bills you pay to national or regional suppliers and all the payments are made by regular debit to your bank account. These will stay as they are and because they are repeating expenses you can keep them with the bank payment method.

It is the discretionary and local spending where you will find it makes a lot of sense to go with the Cash approach and the Envelope System. The most frequent spends will be in food shopping, meals out (including those you buy at work), public transport or taxi fares, pocket money, and clothing.

Withdraw the Cash on your Payday.

If you are weekly paid then you can do this the day you receive your weekly wage. I would suggest you draw out the full amount after tax has been paid and take this money home with you. Sit down at your kitchen table and divide the money into the various envelopes. You don't do this equally, but allocate the cash to each area according to what your weekly spending pattern has been.

If you are paid a monthly salary, then the same situation applies. Draw the cash out and split into the different spending categories according to the amounts you need for the month in each of those separate categories.

Take the envelope when you go to the shops.

As you are setting off to do the weekly food shop, pick up the envelope marked Food or Groceries and do the shop from the cash in there. Place the receipt for the food shop back into the envelope. and add a simple note with the date and amount. This is a handy way to track your food spend by the end of the month.

Of course, cash left over in the envelope at the end of your pay period shows you have made a savings and this means a win that you can transfer to another envelope in a different category, or simply place it into Savings. Enjoy any surplus and see that this still represents you being in control of the spending. Celebrate by holding onto the money left over!

When the money is gone you stop spending!

If there is money in that category you are technically free to spend it. There will be seasonal times when you naturally find yourself buying some warm clothing or new footwear to replace what is no longer wearable. But you are not allowed to take money from one category to spend in another. The whole purpose of setting a budget is to work through it in line with the initial plan you set for yourself.

If you need more money for a category than you budgeted for, ask yourself *"What have I done here?"* or *"How did I miscalculate the money needed for this?"* See it as a valid and helpful learning experience to get the numbers wrong, even slightly miscalculating what you need for the week or the month. Do not then pick up a credit card to pay for more of that expense just because you have used the cash that you had allocated. Instead, **you must learn to go without that expense** or a specific item until the next payday and your refreshing of the envelopes.

A couple of my tenants were paid monthly, but always running out of cash by the end of week three. I sat down with them and explained the envelope system and within two months they had mastered this simple process, showing a small but very positive surplus at the end of the second month, while managing successfully through the first month. It was good to see the increase in their self-esteem as they tackled this challenge together. By placing the cash into envelopes on their payday, and only taking out of the house the money they would need for that intended shopping trip, they steadily learned to curb their lazy spending.

The psychological benefit of handling your money.

The moment you hand over paper and coins to buy something you really do have more attachment to the item. If you are unaware of this, try a simple experiment for yourself. Take out $100 today and only pay cash for items tomorrow when you leave the house. You may have a card with a positive balance on it, a debit card that you can use as a contactless or PIN payment. Tomorrow though, don't use your card. Just pay cash from your wallet or purse. Count the change out and count it back in again with each transaction.

You will likely notice several changes, some more obvious than others. Handing over cash is going to have an impact on the way you shop. You will notice that you second guess yourself when you have to pull out cash instead of just tapping the contactless payment card. You may find yourself asking *"Do I want this?"* or *"How badly do I really need this today?"* Money will very likely move through your hands more slowly when it is real money than when you make a purchase electronically at the till or register.

Make a Shopping List

Some might consider this old fashioned, but drawing up a list of what you are setting out to buy is an action that can save you many hundreds of dollars a month. Simply by thinking through what you need to buy you will cut out the wastage that happens - especially in grocery shopping - when you purchase duplicate items or buy too much of a perishable item that can then go off before you get around to using it.

Leave Your Debit Card at Home.

Just in the beginning of this process of budget mastery, leave your plastic at home. Not for ever and not always, but just for today. Yes, I know this feels weird, but if you are shopping in your neighborhood you know where the card is! Take a moment to understand that you can get through the fear of not being attached to your plastic. You are working with cash right now - just for today - to start to remove your addiction to shopping without thinking about the money being spent.

The process of knowing you are going out for an hour and only taking cash with you can be a real wake-up call. Why? Precisely because it will show you how many times you would otherwise make an impulse buy where you don't give consideration to the process of choosing whether to pull cash out for that purchase.

If this suggestion makes you nervous, you can take a calculator with you as you walk around the shop or use a calculator app on your phone to be absolutely sure you have enough cash with you to comfortably make the grocery purchases and get through the checkout area without feeling embarrassed at a shortfall!

ACTION LEARNING

- When did you last go a week without 'flashing the plastic?'
- Are you scared of handling cash and where might that fear come from?
- Consider the amount of cash you need for the next shop visit?
- Make a SHOPPING LIST of items and stick to it, nothing else.
- Get into a strict habit of ALWAYS asking for a receipt.
- Note all your spending on the envelope itself or in your notebook or phone.

IV

GETTING PRACTICAL

11

GIVE DIRECTION TO EVERY DOLLAR

Every dollar, pound or peso needs a steer in the direction you want it to go. Money will do whatever you tell it to do. This includes buying good quality clothing that will last a long time, decent and healthy food that is good for you, or longer term savings that can grow by benefit of compound interest to become a good retirement fund. Money is equally happy to go on track shoes, burgers, fizzy pop and amusement arcades. Self-help books or comics. Takeaway food on a regular basis or occasional date night meals out. Once it has been spent on something with no future value, there is nothing for you to be getting back from it. It simply follows your instructions.

So how you allocate your spending will have an impact on where you see longer term results or instant and short-term gratification of the need for fast food, quick and disposable clothing, etc. Whether with $50 or $250 you get to choose for yourself where the money is spent. Take time when starting on the design of a spending plan to decide on what works for you, how you receive a benefit from that spend as opposed to using the money elsewhere. Get into the habit each time you are about to spend of asking yourself a simple and easy question as you think about the item. *"What does this spending do for me?"* or a *"How am I really going to benefit from this purchase?"*

Regular themes and categories are going to be the familiar places you know well. You need to pay for the roof over your head, so you have the category of **Accommodation.** You are no good to anyone including yourself without the energy that comes from eating well and so **Food** is a main category. You will need to start monitoring what you spend on food that comes into the house as staples for cooking and making of meals, compared with the amount you spend on takeaways and eating out.

To get to your place of work you might take a bike or perhaps you walk. If you use a vehicle then **Transport** is the category where you consider and log your spend on fuel, insurance, and vehicle finance if you borrowed to buy the car or truck. Transport is obviously the place where you log the cost of your bus travel card, municipal tram or train ticket for the season, but is also where you record the amount you spend on a taxi cab, Lyft, Uber or other paid use of transport during your spending month.

Many people think of a **Holiday** as a cost to be placed on a credit card and then repaid - with the additional interest cost burden - over the subsequent year. This behavior simply adds to your debt burden. Start over with a new approach to being able to save in advance for a short break or a longer vacation Plan for your holiday by identifying your location, method of transport, cost of accommodation. What about the price of meals out at the place you stay or at the resort? How about day trips and excursions while there? You need to have a Holiday category within your planning.

Too often we fail to plan for **Retirement**, after all this is where we are going to spend many years of our life after work and without the salary we might have been enjoying for decades. So, the creation of and the steady contribution to a retirement pot should be the main focus of our longer term savings activities.

Start with building up several short and medium term **Savings** pots for the scale of the imagined problem you might anticipate. You have a service failure on your car and need to lay your hands on $500. This needs to come from a fund you have built up with this level of money set aside. How about a surprise $2,000 bill? Can you manage that by withdrawing money from an account where you have already been saving regularly for unexpected large bills, and without touching any or all of your normal expenditure for the month? Being able to cope with such bills is going to be easier once you start budgeting for them in advance, even when you are unsure what the large bills are going to represent right now.

Giving each dollar a deliberate use this way is a massive aid to your good money management. By directing the flow of money, you will gain more confidence because you know where that money is going, but also you will feel great that you are in control. No more of the 'spend-and-hope' approach for you! Going forward from here you will be aiming to run a **Zero-Based budget**. This simply means that you can identify what happens with each dollar that comes into your account.

Using the phrase zero-based budget can cause confusion. It absolutely does NOT mean you run to having no money in your accounts! This is about knowing that ALL the money you bring in has been directed to a function and has a specific purpose. You might use 88% of your income to pay bills and put 12% into various savings accounts or pots, 6% each into short term savings and 6% into retirement funds.

In a different example you might pay out 72% on the various living expenses and debt servicing, leaving you with 28% for savings and retirement allocation, putting 20% into retirement and 8% to the short term account.

The Zero-based approach to budgeting allows you to track and identify where your money goes and what it does for you, giving you the power of then being able to decide how you want to make any changes in direction next month. Let's say that you allocated 20% of your income last month to the Food category. This month you realize you have plenty of food at home and some money from this category unspent, even after eating out twice since your last salary. What can you do? You could allocate a lesser percentage to food this month, perhaps 15%. The money still left over from last month could go into one of your newly created small balance savings accounts. Or you could take the remaining money and split it equally between debt reduction and savings. Alternatively, how about moving that notional 5% way from Food for this period and pushing it across to Holidays? The choice is with you. By watching what works and noticing where you spend, you have the ultimate freedom to decide how you draw up your spending and allocate that money in the next pay period.

These are just illustrations for the purpose of demonstration. The important thing is that you start to see your spending patterns as Percentages of your income, gaining clarity about the direction you are giving to your money.

ACTION LEARNING

- Make your money do a job and give very clear direction.

- In each transaction be clear about the value your money creates.
- How do you feel knowing that every dollar has a specific place to go?
- You are in control of your money and not the other way around!

12

EVERY MONTH IS DIFFERENT

This can be crippling for you to ignore. The calendar contains months of different lengths. The seasons vary in temperature and are no friend to you in winter when you need to budget and pay for heating bills or the height of summer when air con can reduce your account balance literally as you watch the mercury level rise in your temperature gauge. National holidays, religious festivals, public holidays and family get togethers or anniversary celebrations can seriously deplete your funds.

You must know the phrase *'Every day is a school day'*. I first heard this in my workplace a couple of years ago. The reference is to us learning something every day and so the phrase works well as a reminder that in personal finance just as in life, we regularly get to learn something new. We should always be open to learning something new. There are never two days that are identical. So, it is with income and costs. Your pay might be exactly the same month after month, but this pattern is never true of spending! Hence the potential for a challenge!

In some parts of the country you need to allow for winter

tires, snow chains, and bad weather vehicle checks. In another extreme you have to consider the additional costs for a change in lighting during long and dark winters. Some experience hurricane season, others suffer with torrential rain and flood risk! The days change around us and with these we need to shift and adapt ourselves to meet the financial requirements.

As a residential landlord I have always been surprised when most tenants think there are just 4 weeks in a month. For sure this is true of a rare 28 day month, but what about the month that carries 31 days? The easiest way to look at this is to see that a 31 day month is actually 4.42 weeks and to plan your money spending accordingly. (The geeks will be happy with this detail, but you can just simplify and realize that you need to let your money stretch to cover the longer months!). You might get really into this and find that in a short month you do see a balance left over and in the longer month less surplus is left for you on the final day.

Some of my residents or lodgers in our houses receive state benefit support either for their accommodation monies or for their living costs or for both. There is an option to receive their living money every two weeks and those who struggled with budgeting monthly, definitely find it easier to be paid every two weeks and receive 26 payments in a year. This process of being more mindful of the way they consider their money - and being strict about how long they need to make it last until the next payment - certainly helps them to retain better control of their cash and spending.

Be mindful of the need to consider your personal budget for the month ahead according to such factors as the length of the month, the date you get paid, the number of birthdays, holidays or national vacation days in the calendar and whether any of your smaller number of annual payments fall in this given month.

The variety within the year is a great reason to work at your budget to include money you direct into savings pots. This way you are gradually creating money reserves that will see you able to cope with change. Expect change. Anticipate a potential financial surprise. Build your savings and be prepared!

13

FOCUS ON THE IMPORTANT CATEGORIES

WHEN YOU HAVE MADE THE DECISION TO PAY YOURSELF FIRST - and then committed to this as a habit - saving money moves from last to first place in your priorities. Stephen Covey was an amazing thinker and speaker. His book "Seven Habits of Highly Effective People" is one that has positively influenced the lives of millions of people and continues to do so. The first habit is called 'Begin with the End in Mind' and is a powerful tool for bringing about the change that you want to see.

As you start this process of taking control of your money make sure you begin with the most important elements first. From my perspective these are about ensuring that you are safe and have some level of protection for unexpected amounts that require paying.

Pay Yourself First (PYF).

We could pretend that you don't need to start saving, but would be kidding only yourself. Make use of **Pay Yourself First** as a way to protect yourself and those you care about against difficult financial situations. Allocating money to savings before any other category of spending is how you reward yourself for the effort and planning in becoming financially more secure. This should be the basic rule of money management, that you need to build a financial buffer around yourself for those inevitable demands on your funds which will happen regularly but often in a way that is unpredictable.

So, the first category must be **Savings** as an essential element of your budget. After this come the Four Basics of Food, Accommodation, Clothing and Transport.

Please give me permission to paint you a very extreme picture to illustrate how the categories of basic budgeting connect and interlock. Look at it like this. If you have no financial Savings buffer to protect yourself, then the loss of your job could lead to the loss of your home and you would be in dire straits very quickly. Without **Accommodation** and the associated utilities spend you will find it difficult to register for social security, to engage with people via traditional mail options, be unable to host friends, could risk homelessness as a real status, and struggle to find work. If you have no fund for **Food** and eating regularly, you are unlikely to have the physical and mental health needed to attend work, hold down that job, feed yourself or family, and so many aspects of your personal life will fall apart. **Clothing** means you can go out into the world, engage socially and in a workplace with the appropriate garments and earn money as you work and connect with other people.

The **Transport** aspect of your budget is tied to employment, to getting your children to school, clubs and activities, to reaching the grocery stores and the DIY shops. It is your route to visiting friends and family and sustaining a social life which supports your well-being and mental health. This doesn't need to be a vehicle or a car. It can easily be public transport where that network is good, reliable and regular. During the first six months of the COVID-19 pandemic and the mass trend of people working from home where possible, I had very little use for my car. My mileage driven was down by ca 80%. The savings on fuel acted as a real boost to my bank balance. When I needed to travel, I used the train system for a few hours a week and really enjoyed this.

Can you be thoughtful and reduce your transport costs? If you have two vehicles can you manage with just one, cutting your spend on fuel, insurance and maintenance, giving an injection to long term savings? If you have a vehicle on finance and are paying monthly interest on this, then could you trade down and get a car without finance, a significantly older model that still gets you to where you want to be, but without the $450 a month being paid for this?

My apologies to you for the bleakness of this. If it seems too harsh please just stop to consider that so many people are only two or three months away from having no money at all. It works for the banks to have us all in debt or with low levels of savings, because we are then vulnerable to them and their ability to 'help' us with further loans. Do yourself a massive favor and build your cash reserves and long term savings. Accumulating cash reserves really is the strongest way forward to change your circumstances and this brings us back to why you should place Savings as your very first priority each time funds come in. This is the real benefit of Paying Yourself First.

ACTION LEARNING

- This budget journey belongs to you.
- Pay Yourself First and then pay the bills.
- Know your numbers and pay the bills after contributing to saving.

14

PROTECT ONE CARD

There are promoters out there of the idea that if you have any debt you should cut up all your credit cards and end any and all credit facilities. The potential weakness of this perspective is that it treats adults like children who have no financial discipline, little determination to work with a steady plan to boost savings and also pay down debt. To only pay debts from the surplus on your budget, leaves you completely vulnerable to illness, job loss, or any other distraction that cuts, damages or entirely removes your earning ability.

If this perspective from some of the 'debt and money camps' is about getting rid of all cards I think the guidance is flawed. Even if you are a spender and have got into serious debt on plastic, I think you should have one card. Not to use all the time, especially if you have some impulsive habits around shopping, but as a protection, as a form of ID and as a tool for credit repair if this is something you want to look at and monitor over time. Or you use it every week and completely clear the spending value on it every two weeks. If you want to you can use the card several times a week with your shopping process and then each weekend transfer the amount of the borrowing to the card account and have a clear balance again.

Right now, I want to suggest that you maintain one card as a useful buying tool. Not necessarily for everyday use and certainly not to the point where you binge on it and then struggle to clear it at month end.

If you are a chronic 'over-spender', unable to manage the clearing of a card, have the card but give it to a friend to look after it for you. At least for this first stage of creating your spending plan. It can be a common trap when embarking on the credit repair journey, of getting yourself a low balance card with perhaps a $500 balance on it. You intend to spend a bit and pay it off in full. You can guess what often happens! You spend $497 in the first two months and for the next two years are stuck paying just a minimum amount. In an example like this the balance stays close to the limit and your credit rating sucks.

An easy alternative to this is to set up a weekly automated bank payment and watch the balance fall back to zero. Using a card this way can see the balances increased by the lender. Make a few purchases on the card, and the same week make a full payment with a bank transfer to the card account. The credit rating is maintained, and you have an available instrument or tool to support your financial journey. It can also serve to act as an intelligent approach for those occasions when you think you want to protect perhaps the purchase of an electrical item with warranties, to reserve a hotel stay or buy an air ticket in advance.

Used sensibly and paid off in full each time, just the one card is quite enough. Why? Because you are using cash and automated payments for the other transactions.

. . .

ACTION LEARNING

- Allow for seasonal needs within your budget calculations.
- Anticipate your spending rather than be surprised by it!
- Protect the main spending categories within your budget, redirecting the surplus to savings.
- Maintain some credit facilities to give yourself flexibility, not to carry as debt.

15

THE 'NO SPEND' CHALLENGE DAY

BEING SHORT ON CASH, BROKE AND IN DEBT ARE ALL situations that you want to move away from. It hurts like hell to not be able to pay for a birthday present for your kids or to buy a snack at the cinema after the high cost of those damn tickets. Managing your income and expenditure with thought and attention to detail is a sensible thing to do at any stage in life, we all know this as true.

However, when you are really low on funds, it is a right royal pain in the butt to think that a friend or work colleague has invited you to a social event in a bar or restaurant where you just know that it would be a financial melt-down for you to attend and spend money! To make things better in the longer term there really are things you can do right now to know those improvements are just around the corner.

Before today, you may well have been annoyed, depressed, aching to your bones over the financial troubles you are facing. Crying under the pressure of having a job and being paid, yet having absolutely nothing to show for this work at the end of the month! Your money comes in and is almost instantly gone when all those automated payments come directly out of your bank account. To see the money land and for it all to have gone within the space of a few days, this hurts so much! I spent several years like this myself, sleeping badly for fear of the bills arriving in the morning post and worrying about being unable to make a payment.

Learning about the principle of Paying Yourself First can truly be a habit changing wake-up call, a real 'light bulb' moment. Well, here's another one for you that can change your financial thinking and significantly boost your bank account.

I encourage you to start today with a new habit, and to help you understand that the establishment of a habit can be sorted within 30 days of repetition. Your brain is so used to going out and accepting your spending instructions that it will take a while for it to accept the decision you made to cut costs and build savings through intelligent budgeting. You could try and pretend you have no damaging spending habits, but your brain has been getting used to the idea. You might need a while to change that stinking thinking!

Here is your instruction for today.

"Today you do not spend on anything at all."

That's it. Today you will not spend any money. You are certainly not adding to your debt, and this alone is reason to celebrate! More than this though, today will be a day where you take on no new cost. Your do not spend. You do not handover any money or pay a bill.

- You do not drop $5 to get a coffee on the high street. Instead you make your own from the jar you have in the kitchen. If this is a working day you take in a flask of your own.
- You do not need the grocery store today you have enough unused food items at home.

- You do not accept a cinema invite from a friend unless they are buying the ticket and you can take your own snacks with you in your pocket.

Today you will not be spending. Not one penny. Not one cent of spending. There are utility bills to pay and they can wait one day, and you can make a payment tomorrow. You may already have them set up at the bank on autopay.

Your Needs are Met.

I'm not asking you to lock yourself in your room and withdraw from life! Just saying that you are not going to spend money today. Be clear on the difference.

You have all the basics in place. You know the truth of what has been written earlier about you already having everything you need to survive. You have somewhere to sleep tonight, clothes to wear and you've eaten. Sorted!

This is only about today. Tomorrow is not here yet, so let's not consider a day beyond this. Today is about making a massive, powerful, but incredibly simple shift in your money thinking and your behavior.

Your brain will likely be in turmoil at this final decision. Your excuses will be starting to fly thick and fast.

Beware of excuses.

Excuses and random thoughts like:

- "But I need to pay my gym membership today."
- "But I have to buy some milk."
- "But the bank has told me to settle my credit card in full this month ..."
- "But I need to ..."

These are all comments made in denial of the basic truth that you are in a mess and need to get yourself out of it. I've heard them all before and have tried a few of them myself.

Your subconscious mind might be playing a game with you right now and making suggestions that are unhelpful and downright unwanted. They can go something like these.

"I want to go into town and buy some clothes."

You already have a mass of clothes you never wear and plenty of items and outfits that you are quite happy with. Today you are spending nothing at all, let alone on clothing.

"I want to borrow money from the department store to finance a new television."

You have a phone so watch a movie on that. There is a fully functioning laptop in your house so make use of it to watch a free streaming channel and choose a film that you can settle down and enjoy. The last thing you need is easy access credit and an agreement to take on debt, especially for something so pointless as an upgraded TV screen!

"I need to nip over to the bookstore and order the hot new title that I read about."

Err, no you don't! You can get yourself into the library and borrow it for free. If it's already out on loan, simply get your name down on the list and get ready for it to be available next week. You can swap a book with a friend. You probably have ten unread books in your home. Coming from a book hoarder like me, this number is probably closer to a hundred unread books or more - but let's keep that as a secret between friends! You do not need to buy a book! Instead you deliberately choose to spend nothing today.

If any of the thoughts that voice themselves were actually significant you could take the cash out of a savings account and walk into a thrift store and buy a really decent used TV, or into the library and get a different book, one that is at least similar to the new one you are keen about. Your mind will play all manner of tricks on you to suggest, imply or trick you into thinking you need the new, the trending or the must-have item. Face the facts. Wanting them is not the same as needing them. Every time you resist the urge to spend you are winning by keeping money in your account for another day.

So, stick with your promise to yourself.

"Today, for this one day, I will not spend."

You can have friends around for a meal. You can enjoy a bike ride. You can visit a gallery. You can enjoy a visit to a thrift shop. You can walk around a store and browse all manner of gorgeous items, resisting the urge to buy anything. You can go through the city center and take a picnic with you. You can take a pack of cards into the square and play patience or meet a friend for a game. You can walk around your neighborhood and chat with neighbors.

How about an hour with a good book? Fancy watching a movie? Look online and find a new batch of articles on a topic or skill set you want to learn about. Can you give an hour to tidying the cellar or sorting out the children toys? What about grabbing some pencils and taking half an hour to try out drawing whatever you see out of the windows?

One major element of committing to a No Spend Day is that you stop to think about what you can do for free. In the process you might start to see how much you spend while attempting to entertain yourself when you can actually look after yourself without spending a dime today.

I am not asking you to have one No Spend Day after another. But what could happen if you get used to the idea of a couple of days every month where you find your own food without going to a cafe, where you download a book for free instead of buying a new one, or you make time for a visit to the town museum or library armed with a notebook and a flask of coffee, saving money as you enjoy a new activity that is fun?

It really is as easy as this to make your money last longer and go further. You make a date with yourself for a No Spend Day. You can get friends and family involved, explaining to them what the benefits are. If you are doing this just for yourself, you have total choice over the agenda and the options considered. Otherwise you get to take a vote on where you go and what you do as a household or a friendship group.

To put things really simply, your money situation only becomes worse for three core reasons:

1. Your cost of living goes up because you increase your commitment to spending and to debt, or

2. Your income goes down and your costs remain the same, or

3. Your costs go up AND your income goes down.

Here we are looking at a No Spend Day as an effective way for money to stay with you for a day longer. Sometimes this will mean you gain an extra day within your week or month, and this gives you the real opportunity to have that money added to what you might normally save in a month. You have cut back on spending for a whole day, giving yourself the potential for your bank account to be stronger after that day has ended.

What Might a No Spend Day look like in reality?

You have fuel in your car, so you don't need to buy more. You have food in your kitchen cupboards, so you eat from what you have. You have books on your shelves, paper in your printer, credit on your phone, clothes in your wardrobe, electric, gas and water supply to your house and water supply to your property. So why would you need to spend anything? You don't.

You might have a social gathering to attend. You can attend, with the proviso that no spending is involved. Popping over to a neighbor's for coffee meets this situation, but going out for lunch with a friend doesn't. In a situation where you get such an invite you can be honest.

Just say *"Actually, I've committed to a No Spend Day today, so will have to say Thanks but No thanks"* and decline based on this. Don't be surprised when your friend asks you about the No Spend Day.

Or you could simply say, "I would love to meet up, but right now I'm committed to something else. Let's arrange for next month."

This is your money we are talking about. Remember that money always follows your instruction. Your goal is to save where you can and cut costs each time you have the chance to do so. This way you get to see your balances grow at the bank, but more importantly you have the peace of mind which comes from knowing that you are making sure your outgoings are less than your income. Having a regular No Spend Day is a great way to slow down the flow of money through your hands. It offers you a rest from the addictive pleasures of spending and shopping.

A bill might turn up in the post this morning, but having a bill arrive and needing to pay it are not the same thing. Sure, you will pay it, but not today. Today is about ensuring you have no spending and feel the benefits of this.

You have chosen not to spend money today, all as part of gaining control of your money, so stick with your commitment to yourself. Just for today.

"Today, for this one day, I will not spend."

ACTION LEARNING

- Learn to enjoy a day without spending.
- See a No Spending Day as an opportunity.
- Identify and enjoy cost free activities.

- Prove to yourself that you can break the addiction to Daily Spending.
- Having a bill arrive and having to pay it are not the same thing.
- It's OK to say 'No' to spending and keep hold of your money.

V

MOVING AHEAD

16

DEVELOPING FINANCIAL INDEPENDENCE

WITH HOUSE PRICES SEEMINGLY ALWAYS JUST OUT OF EASY reach and recession of the economy happening in a regular cycle, you need a game plan for increasing your personal and financial resilience. It makes sense to build up your reserves and to strengthen your personal situation where you can. To move closer to financial independence you will need to be driven by clear goals and a hunger for results that motivates you to take daily actions.

As I write we have been through a year damaged by a global pandemic with illness, job losses, the closure of the high street for months at a time and a reluctance to leave home. I notice that a lot of friends who were clearing debt ahead of building their savings before COVID-19 have switched tactics to safeguard cash and continue the debt reduction, but with smaller regular payments than before.

Many young adults have been asking about the issue of dependence upon their parents for financial support, for occasional loans, for the clearing of a debt burden and I want to comment on this as an issue. In most cases such young adults as these are working in an early career or first stable job, but are still facing the burden of student debt, expensive accommodation, high costs of transport to and from work in an urban environment and the constant concern over balancing personal finance.

Let's look closer at this. What are these people spending money on that could be cut or trimmed from their spending? How might they make arrangements with credit providers to reduce ongoing monthly payments to a more manageable level? Is there scope for additional income and where would they find the time and energy levels to achieve this? My concern comes at the lifestyle expectations of young adults. A house of their own, accommodation rented in a trendy area, the 'right' wardrobe or car. Any and all of these can sink you in a heartbeat with interest rate changes, job loss, change or reduction in working hours, the inability of your money to stretch to cover everything.

Financial independence from your parents is not the same thing as financial independence for yourself. Let's be clear on the distinctions between these. The first means that you are making your way in the world without a significant helping hand. If you are in an affordable single bed unit that you rent and a parent visits you and brings a bag of groceries or takes you out for an evening meal, this is one thing. It is completely another to earn $50,000 a year in your job role but have a $60,000 lifestyle and expect your bank of Mom and Dad to bail you out with $1,000 a month. In this case you are dependent upon them for help, and the evidence shows you are not being responsible about balancing your income and your spending. Now is a good time to grow up!

In this situation you are broke and continuing to harm your chances of breaking free to make and control your own spending plan. If you are going to borrow from a family member or a friend, be really clear with them about your own expenses and income. Transparency here will mean you can get help based on the truth, as opposed to borrowing money based on holding back the real numbers from the person who cares about you enough to want to help!

Financial independence in your own right means that you live on less expenses than your regular income, and you also set aside a percentage of all you earn as your route to safe protection over the longer term. Which of the two situations do you want for yourself?

The second type of Financial Independence is the place you reach when you have enough saved and invested that you no longer need to work regularly or at all to pay all your daily expenses. There are stages to go through to reach this retirement level and saving is the common factor in all of these approaches.

You can search for #debtfreecommunity #minimalism and #frugalliving as an introduction to the conversations happening about cutting your costs to the minimum. For most people the largest cost each month is accommodation so anything you can do to reduce this as a percentage of your income allows you to boost your savings significantly, and brings financial peace of mind closer sooner. Living smaller, living with less clutter, living with lower utility costs, all of these are practical ways to go as you seek that financial independence.

How Do I create Financial Independence?

Constant saving and some regular investing will support this goal. You will need to start educating yourself about the routes to achieving this long term goal and you might want to seek help from a qualified financial planner along the way. Certainly, the process of seeking and learning from other perspectives can boost your knowledge and potentially save you a few years through the intelligent use of a portion of your savings for best returns right now.

The first stage is to identify the income required for you

to be free of the need to work. Understand that this is *not* the reason for a book on working to a create an effective budget and a spending plan to match. Becoming financially independent is the natural extension of following the basic rules of saving and investing over time. By developing a specific plan for the income, you need to live comfortably, you can adapt and adjust the level of your longer term saving and budget tightly to boost those same savings at every opportunity.

You are on the Ten Minute Budget journey because you are fed up with not having enough - or anything at all - left over at the end of the month. It hurts you to admit this, yet at the same time you are fully aware that you can get a handle on this. You are committed to turning things around with a simple daily focus on your Ten Minute Budget

Some sacrifices will be necessary to pursue aggressive savings goals, and this is why I mentioned the need to be hungry to achieve your goals and willing to take daily action towards them. I love residential rental activity because it creates both income and accommodation for us. In one house for example, the income from renting out just one spare bedroom professionally (whether on a nightly or weekly basis), is equal to our accommodation cost for that entire building each month. You could take the view that this means we live free of accommodation costs and put nothing into savings, or you could equally see from the angle that we have a spare amount of cash to invest each month that is equal to the accommodation cost which we already cover from our pay check income.

You need to determine what your goals are for a future income and what you are prepared to do to achieve this, potentially saving years off your retirement date because of how you set money aside and cut your costs.

Starting with good saving habits as soon as possible gives

you an advantage that supports you as you move forward. As soon as you can live well within your means you have created the scope for new savings or enhanced savings. Manage your money now rather than leave it until next week. There will come a time when your parents are retired themselves and may not be able to support you with financially help. Instead the tables may turn, and they will require help from you. The world can turn on a penny and you need to be able to adapt to such changes.

ACTION LEARNING

- What spending behavior can you adopt to be more financially frugal?
- How radical can you be in cutting costs in order to create a new surplus?
- What Income and Expense numbers do you need to work with to live happily?
- Identify some specific actions you can take to boost your rate of saving.

17

EASY STEPS TO REDUCE YOUR WORRY

FROM A PLACE OF WORRY IT CAN BE DIFFICULT TO MAKE GOOD financial decisions. The stress of thinking about where to spend your money, how to make it stretch further and how to avoid spending where you can, any and all of these can create difficulty for you.

I sat down with a friend recently because he was seemingly making his decisions based out of fear, instead of coming from a place of consideration and thought. I had seen him buy a car that broke down regularly. In his shopping for food and household supplies he seemed to go from bulk buying one month and seeing a waste of the foods that perished, to then buying almost daily the next month.

Making spending decisions based on how you wake up in the morning is not a great way forward! Heading off to the store without knowing your cashflow is equally going to lead to some foolish purchases that will wreck your intentions for balanced spending or could leave to embarrassment at the checkout when your card is declined.

Consider how any decisions in your life pan out when you make them without any or with only very little thought.

"I must do this now" or *"I have to buy this item today"* are purchasing decisions driven by emotion and short-term feelings, not by any perspective based on what you and your household can afford from your spending plan.

To lurch from one impulse buy, to a bad purchase and then to repeat the behavior achieves nothing except disaster and lack of funds that you have swapped good money for bad items out of poor quality decisions. You are living your financial life like a person attempting to cross wild country without a map or compass. You will get confused, lost and will have to face real risk. Instead you can identify ways that will work for you so that you don't continue like this and find a better, safer path going forward from here. When you operate out of fear with your spending you are potentially - not definitely - going to make purchases you will regret later.

Developing good habits for where your money goes, this comes best from a place where you are not in panic, where you can think through the large purchases and make time to work out where they will come in your spending. Wisely made long-term decisions can often be better than those short-term and knee-jerk reactions that come from the fear in the pit of your stomach which can be a companion of debt and financial overload. Having a knowledge of your numbers puts you in a place of better-informed decision making.

How Can I tell if I am Fearful?

Here are some telltale signs that you might be functioning from a place of fear.

- Do you catch yourself with thoughts like these, perhaps even saying them aloud to yourself?
- I am forever counting the days until my next payday.
- In the grocery store I am always anxious when I present my payment card.

- I feel awkward and ashamed when others talk about having savings.
- The thought of bad news scares me in case I need to pay emergency bills.
- When the mail arrives, I am scared to open the envelopes.
- My money only lasts a few days from payday.
- I am nervous I might be laid off at work when they announce simple cost cutting.
- How to Step away from being driven by Fear

It is a dangerous place to be, living on the edge like this and you need to quickly get a handle on it. Your wallet is empty, there is nothing in your purse and there is no spending power behind the cards you have. Your account has very little in it and no short-term overdraft or borrowing facility from the bank. Lacking any savings, you feel like you are stuck between the proverbial 'rock and a hard place' with no spare room to operate from.

Knowing this is where you are, you must take action in two areas in order to give yourself breathing space and a realistic strategy for recovery. Neither of them is difficult, but each will require you to think differently in order to get new results.

First, you have to monitor your costs and understand why you are spending more than you have as income. You are going to need to take the medicine, no matter how bitter it might taste to begin with. Addicted to spending money on things that you cannot afford to be buying you are going to need to start being less impulsive, more thoughtful and SPEND LESS THAN YOU EARN.

In those four words is the secret to becoming financially secure. Let me say it to you again just for impact :) SPEND LESS THAN YOU EARN! Now, please don't tell me that you don't already know this. I am going to ask you to get your thinking straight about this and remind you here of some of the actions you can take to track and monitor your spending. You have to become more consciously aware of the stinking thinking that has been holding you in this awful place of lack and struggle.

Second, you are going to start building a money buffer between you and the world you live and breathe in. A buffer is a safe place, a protection, a way of ensuring you can always function financially when a surprise, an emergency or an otherwise unplanned for expense needs to be covered.

How you start the creation of the buffer is a thing you get to determine all on your own, but the importance of this is something I want you to get your head around very quickly. You can put a percentage of what you earn to one side with a virtual 'Do Not Touch!' label on it. This is money that you build up by regular contributions and which you regard as almost sacred. It works like this: You get paid weekly or monthly and you immediately transfer 10% of your wage into a separate account. The 90% remaining in your current account to checking account, this is yours to work with and use over the next week or month. But you absolutely cannot and must not attempt to touch the 10% that you squirrelled away.

The next time you receive your wage or salary you again set aside 10% as soon as the money lands in your account. You can see that it only takes ten weeks on this model to have a full week of income sitting untouched in your Savings account. If you are paid monthly, it will obviously take ten months to accumulate the equivalent of a one month salary. If you double the savings proportion to 20% of earned income, then after five months you have a whole month of living income saved as a buffer.

Put Your Budget to WORK!

Begin with a very basic budget where you identify the minimum send you need to live and cover your accommodation, food and transport. By cutting back on any spending other than the essentials you will naturally see a surplus that goes into your savings. It can often be helpful to set up a few small accounts with the title or name of Emergency Account and each with a different value, for example start saving in one until you have $500. Your next target is a second savings account that you build up $1,000 and again you don't touch the month. After this a third account might have a goal of you collecting together $5,000. Achieving your very first balance of $500 will feel like such a positive result and spur you on to greater savings and becoming more inventive about how and where you cut your costs and boost your savings balances.

After a couple of months working to a tight, basics-only budget with your shopping you will be so much more aware of the patterns of spending - impulsive and considered - by which money flows through your hands. Tracking and counting this spending over the first two months will give you so much more insight into your money behavior, but by the end of it you should be able to fully trust yourself to save, to spend frugally and only where necessary. Play with the numbers and set yourself a percentage savings figure that matches with and supports your defined saving goals.

After this you are ready to run a more thoughtful and predictable cycle of saving and spending, seeing the balance of your savings accounts grow steadily because you have taken control and said to yourself: *'I will no longer debt!'* or *'I will no longer overspend.'*

From this position of better financial well-being you can more clearly see whether the problems you have been facing were as a result of overspending, creating debt or not earning enough money. It could be you notice that you have suffered due to a combination of all three of the patterns presenting together in your financial circumstances.

Increase Your Take-Home Income

Think of where you are now. If you don't make radical change in the form of cutting your spending, you are going to continue to suffer. By not looking at ways to boost your income you are settling for more of the same and you can barely manage with what you have right now. Something has to give if you are to break free of this cycle of struggle.

Remember that phrase we introduced earlier in this book?

"To know and not to do is not to know."

Your numbers will tell you what needs to be done. For example, if you cut your costs for two months, stop your impulsive spending and find that your bank account balance is growing at a rate you are pleased with, this might be a good enough place for you. Yet if the balance is only growing slightly and your debt burden is not really being touched or reduced in any meaningful way after such cost cutting actions, then bringing in more money is how you are going to beat the cycle of money in, money out and ongoing struggle.

A second job might be all you need, an extra ten hours a week. You might want to stay in the company where you are but gain a new external qualification that will allow you to apply for a better paid role here or in another organization. Better skills can often mean a lift in income, just be sure not to increase your home expenses.

Millions of people generate an extra $500 or $1,000 a month from simple side hustles. Tree felling, car washing, driving for Lyft or Uber, working at Dash, or Deliveroo. Coaching and mentoring online, teaching people in the use of musical instruments, car mechanics, software usage or design skills, painting, human modelling, sculpture. House cleaning and vehicle detailing. Home cooking, baking. Market gardening. Babysitting. Yard clearance. Selling on Esty, eBay, Amazon and a ton of other platforms for personal sales is a straightforward process in these vast and well established ventures.

Quite aside from writing new books, I love selling vintage books online. I can average $150 to $200 a week with about two hours work, so will continue to do this as long as people keep buying. My profits are ca 85% so I am happy with it, being paid well for something a hobby I adore.

Find a side gig, a second income, and stick at it. If the main employment or job you have is not something you really enjoy, I would encourage you to at least get satisfaction in the other earning activity, or you will drain yourself emotionally chasing the extra money.

ACTION LEARNING

- How enjoyable is the Ten Minute Daily Budget?
- Can you see a link between knowing your numbers and a lowering of worry and anxiety levels?
- Are your growing your household income where feasible, and doing this without adding stress?
- Each day simply ask yourself *"Where can I not spend today?"*

18

SET UP FOR SUCCESS

THIS IS NOT A SPRINT, BUT A LONG DISTANCE GAME. IN sorting out a spending plan that you can own and enjoy for the benefits it brings, you will need to adopt a long term view. Right now, there could still be panic and overwhelm about whether you will ever get your head around this. Trust yourself! You are going to take simple steps so that each week for just the next two months you actively record and track your income and spending. Just ten minutes a day for tracking and budgeting will give you so much potential for positive financial change. You are putting yourself in control of your money.

You want to gain insight into where the money goes and once you have a sense of this you are able to make the course adjustments that will help you step back from worry. Right now, take simple steps and don't beat yourself up about how you are going to sort out your finances in one go. It is not going to happen this way! Life is not like this and you need to get wise to the fact. One of the biggest reasons for us to struggle with personal finance is not being realistic, refusing to work with the facts of our situation.

Instead you will start to look for simple savings. Can you spend $90 on your weekly food shop rather than $100? If you buy 10 coffees from take away shops or cafes as you travel in and out of work in a week, can you buy just 5 the next week and save yourself $30 in the process? The goal for the two months is to buy none at all, make and carry your own and see the cash staying in your account.

Where you might have been used to a regular trip to the cinema as a family every month, are you really going to notice a shift to every two months in order to cut your costs by a decent $150 when considering the savings on tickets, food, drinks and possibly parking costs that you save? Over a year the six movie nights you cut mean that $900 stays in your account.

These are simple examples and in each one you can adapt to record a reduction in your spending.

Feel confident in looking at every category of both regular and occasional or annual spending and see where you can slice or trim a percentage of each outgoing. This simple act, when repeated, will change your outlook and your confidence as your savings grow.

This book is about you and your household. The numbers that matter are your numbers. So, as you track your daily and weekly spending in order to be clear on your actual numbers, avoid the distraction of what someone else might be doing. When the process seems too much for you, take a break but don't break the new practice of cutting costs. Continue to make savings in your spending, but only at the level that you are comfy with right now. You are looking to create something better for yourself so you can only do this at your own pace. Ten minutes a day is a small investment of time to put you back in the driving seat.

We all live in our own little bubbles of interaction and behavior, so stick with what you know. Maintain some aspects of what you are comfortable with as a lifestyle. Notice how you need to adjust very little to achieve some actually quite significant reductions in the spending that you have been doing unconsciously up till now. Shaving a few dollars off every $100 that you have habitually spent on your activities and purchases will very quickly add up to a good cutting of your regular expenditure.

This process is not intended to be so drastic that it causes you further anguish and stress. Your positive action though is needed in order for you to see a marked change in your finances after a month has passed and then to continue this for a second month of trimming and cutting. Such actions will allow you to sense the good emotional gains of your work. Don't feel the need to adjust anything other than making sure your spending consistently goes down while your income stays the same or gets better.

In this reduction of costs as a percentage of income is the solution you have been looking for. Your first task is to create an obvious gap between your Income and your Expenses, and then to expand this positively. The monetary results you create are yours to keep in the form of reward that you get to allocate to long term Savings and to a Short Term Emergency Fund that will protect you.

Take your time each week to look at where you can reduce your costs. Each month bolster your savings accounts with the benefit of what you have achieved.

ACTION LEARNING

- Have you opened at least one long-term Savings account and one for the short-term?
- What cost cutting actions can you take inside your budget - right now - to see regular units of $100 transferred into a Savings account?

- Always track your Weekly and also Monthly spending.
- Monitor the percentage of earnings that is transferred each payday to Savings.
- Protect yourself with a Large Expenses account as a buffer for those 'unexpected' bills.

VI

LOOKING AFTER YOU

19

THIS IS ONLY ABOUT YOU

IF YOU WANT TO BEAT YOURSELF UP THEN YOU CAN WASTE hours looking at someone else's media posts, brags and flash vehicles. You have something much better to be getting on with! Look instead at your numbers and the way money comes into and out of your life. There is nothing to be gained from comparison, unless it is from a trusted source who can help you from their own experience of learning to handle finance differently and better.

In the past I have certainly been pulled off track a few times by looking at the other person's apparent lifestyle, posts and holiday snaps. None of this matters. What is important are *your* situations and *your* payment patterns. If you are paid weekly, run with a weekly plan on your money. Just repeat this week after week until your get a handle on the finance that puts you in control of where your money needs to be. If you have a monthly salary use this as the way you construct your model. Ten minutes a day is all it takes to create new results.

Where finances might be very tight when you start with the program, then creating a weekly spending plan, and making use of the 'Envelope' concept - whether with real physical envelopes or virtual digital ones - is a powerful way forward. On the day you get your pay check or salary money into your bank account, leave enough money in to cover your regular bank paid bills and draw the rest as cash, splitting it among four envelopes for each of the upcoming weeks until your next pay check is deposited. This cash is for fresh food and consumables such as milk or yoghurt, vegetables, fruit and bread. It is what you would use for coffee or a sandwich during your working day unless you have chosen to boost your accounts by making homemade meals and taking these with you. It is for parking fees, a travel ticket, or the bar of chocolate you think is essential. If you spend all the money from that envelope or the theme for that allocation of your cash, you have to go without for a few days until the start of the next pay period and you repeat the process, this time working to manage the money better and with less impulse shopping.

Again, this is about your situation and there is no 'one size fits all' approach to getting back in control of your money. If you work a main job plus one, or even two extra jobs, you run your spending plan to those paid roles. If you get occasional overtime, be careful that you do not get used to calculating this as repeat or regular income for dividing between the envelopes!

This is only about you and your personal situation.

Focus on the income you have and whether there is scope to increase this. In the short term this additional income might come from an extra job, a side hustle, a source of other earning that you can fit in alongside your main work. In the longer term it could mean a new and better paid job where you work the same hours but for a better take-home paycheck. Keep cutting your costs where you can and diverting a steady percentage to savings accounts, one for emergencies and the other for retirement. These are the two accounts that are going to create your peace of mind very quickly and your financial independence over the years.

Keep your mind on why you are working hard to cut debt, build a financial buffer for your own protection and give yourself to look forward to a paid-for retirement. When you are living hand to mouth, struggling to pay utilities and put food on the table, you can forget the bigger picture. Don't lose sight of why you are engaged in looking at your finances in brief for a few minutes each day. Keep your eyes on the prize of being in control and knowing how good this will feel to you.

- Keep your eyes on your own goals.
- Know why you are accepting the budget challenge and what it represents to you, both financially and emotionally.
- Employ all the techniques you are comfortable with and discard anything else.

20

HAVE WORTHWHILE GOALS

Working endlessly and without a goal to maintain your focus is simply drudgery. The same work, with a specific focus in mind at the end of it, provides you with a completely different way of looking at the work you are putting in. Meaningful goals will energize you as you persist and craft a good budget, one that works for you and allows you to get ahead of the previous troubles.

If you love clothes and have not boosted your wardrobe this past year, you can see and actually feel the strong motivation that comes from saving up $500 into a separate account for rewarding yourself for something achieved. Perhaps you reduce your debt by $5,000 and take the $500 to buy something special which you know you can enjoy wearing for several years. You absolutely understand emotionally that wearing that item will remind you of the work you put in, the sacrifices you made and the results you achieved along the way.

Choose how you reward yourself for a future accomplishment. It could be clothes, a watch, a weekend trip away.

Make the goal something that you are motivated towards with each action you take and each step you make along the journey of enhancing your finances.

When things are tough and you are having a bad day seeing any sense in your personal finance, reminding yourself of the future goal is a way to stay on track. You have made a commitment to making sense of your money and paying down debt while also building up your savings. It will not all be plain sailing, so make sure that you have something that you can hold up on such difficult days and use as a reminder that you have chosen to work through this.

The reward that you buy as a 'Well done!' gesture to yourself does not have to massive, but it does need to mean something to you. You did the work and made the effort with your personal finance. You took the steady steps every week to get your budget in order and have worked your spending plan in a way that is successful for you, so it's completely OK to give yourself a small treat.

Even before you make the big progress, is there something you can motivate yourself with that costs very little? A friend stayed in a mountain hotel with her parents when she was a child and has great memories of the time there on vacation. When she recently had a chance to visit the area as an adult she went to the same resort and picked up a brochure from the staff on the front desk. While she was there, she took one of the attractive complimentary pens for guests. She walked around the resort, enjoyed the pathways through the grounds and past the swimming pools and made a commitment to return and bring her own family once the finances are in better order. Every day she has the pen on her desk, and the pictures she has cut from the brochure and placed on her wall, as simple and yet powerful visual reminders of the goal.

Find something as easy as this and use it to drive you forward with actions that get results for you one day at a time. Whether you're paying off student loans, building up your emergency fund, or paying off your mortgage, you need to focus on your why. What's the reason you're making these sacrifices?

Make the goal setting a powerful thing. I was having coffee with a friend recently and were chatting about goals and how these helped each of us to pay down debt, build savings and have the spending plan in place that works. He mentioned the importance of having a goal that almost hurts you to be chasing after, one that you absolutely have to achieve. I casually said something along the lines of:

"I know exactly what you mean. Having 'a why that makes you cry'!"

We laughed at the image and yet we knew exactly what that meant. Find something that - if you didn't achieve it or didn't bring this result home for your household - would hurt you so much it would make you cry.

A well-chosen goal, one that you are hungry for, is the result of lots of little actions that you follow through with and chase up. On their own each thing can seem small and almost inconsequential. Together they add up to a personal accomplishment that can be incredible in what it gives you.

So set some goals, make them worth working for, give yourself that element of stretch and then just do the work, all the time keeping your eye on the prize.

ACTION LEARNING

- Track your progress to goals that you are achieving for yourself.

- Keep looking at your numbers to remind yourself how far you have come.
- Develop a 'why that makes you cry' as a trigger for taking action.

GO EASY ON YOURSELF

HOW MANY THINGS DID YOU EVER TRY AND GET RIGHT THE first time? Very few, I'm guessing? Did you jump in the swimming pool and move smoothly across to the other side without swallowing water or going under for a few seconds? When you first went on a jog around the neighborhood in your running gear, did you find perfect coordination between muscles, arms and your breathing? Of course not. New habits need time to be practiced before they become second nature.

You want to sort your finances, start to save, clear your bills, have money set aside when a cash challenge presents itself or when a more serious 'financial storm' strikes. You probably also want the emotional peace of knowing that whatever life throws at you there is a way to deal with the problem and bounce back without being completely knocked over by it.

So, when you approach the goal of having your money be 'sorted' is it fair to yourself to expect this to be done, finished, completed or sorted tomorrow? Of course not!

If you put so much pressure on yourself to get everything

tidied up the first week, all you are doing is getting ready for a more painful time in week three or week six when something happens that you had not considered, have not planned around and had built no reserve for. You don't need to do this.

Instead, ease yourself in slowly to building a budget that works for you and your household. Today just grab a coffee or a juice and sit down on your couch to simply think about what you spent money on last week and this week. Jot down the numbers. Test them, add them up. Look at the income you brought in last week compared to the money that you spent and the money left over in your bank account and as cash in your wallet, purse, back pocket or in the tin above the microwave!

There will be receipts for things you forgot to include in your calculations. There will be a couple of $10 bills in the candy jar, $50 in the bedside table and maybe $500 in your checking account. To begin with all you need to do is look at the numbers and the spending. As you review it more closely you will see patterns. How much are you spending on food at work or out of the house meals and coffee. You will spot what money you drop on data updates to your phone, on gaming or competition apps. These seem innocent when you think it is just $1 or $2 here and there, but which can easily add up to $50 in the month. You will see that you forget to buy a monthly travel pass and instead spend more than you needed by buying daily bus or train tickets. You might see that every now and again you get a parking ticket and take too long to pay it, even though the city gives you a reduction for paying with 15 days, you never get around to paying until after the deadline for the discount. these are the patterns you are looking to find in your first sessions of 'dipping your toes into the financial waters that surround you! Don't over think the process.

Make it something you can become familiar with of course, because you are going to be doing this every week until it becomes a natural and instinctive behavior. More than this, make it a behavior that is something you start to enjoy because you get real value from getting in control. Financial value of course because this is about sorting your cash, but emotional value because it allows you to put down the fear levels, to reduce the anxiety week by week. Stick with the Ten Minute Budget as a short daily activity.

It is going to take you at least two whole months, possibly as much as three or four, to get your head around the creation of a spending plan to match your budget. There will be plenty of mistakes along the way as you learn. Why might it take this long to create a real and substantial change that you can continue with happily? Because you have for years been spending more than you earn, simply using up all the money you earn and excluding any creation of a surplus. To achieve what is proposed here within Ten Minute Budget the process needs time to bed down and to be accepted by your brain. You have been running a story in your head for a long time that it is OK to spend every dollar that you earn, even though some important categories such as Saving, Retirement and Large Expenses have not been included within your behaviors. This is what you are dealing with, so it's normal to take a while to adopt some new ways of looking at your money, even the process of being brave enough to work through the numbers and creating your budget!

Take your time. There is no pressure to rush. Tread softly as you explore your spending to begin with and be gentle on yourself. Develop the vision to know where you want to get to in the creation of a budget that will deliver your needs. Have the grace to know what is right as you move forward.

This money journey is one that you control, giving

precise direction to every dollar that comes your way. You've got this one day at a time. Ten minutes at a time.

ACTION LEARNING

- Making mistakes is a part of life. What matters is how you learn to recover and self-correct.
- Steady steps every day will give results you can measure and consider.
- Notice how much better you feel at directing your own money.
- Acknowledge the importance of knowing your numbers and seeing how they can work against you or be completely for you.
- Keep a journal of your progress, noting the inevitable mistakes, but also every win.
- Be proud of yourself for each step taken.
- Share the principles of the Ten Minute Budget with one other person and help them gain control.

ABOUT THE AUTHOR

Collector of books, fan of new reading and ever fascinated with the power of the written world to bring new ideas and thinking.

As an author I love time spent at my desk in my dedicated writing shed at the bottom of the garden or at a table in a neighbourhood coffee shop. I love to be with pens and paper working through ideas for a manuscript or a presentation.

Best of all is getting a concept out of my head and into a conversation with a reader, discussing our different ways of approaching something which unites all of us. This could be around Financial Thinking and Personal Budgeting, dealing with the Clutter we accumulate in our living spaces or wanting solutions and new ways of thinking about Debt so that we can enjoy more control of our money on the way to financial peace of mind.

It is so great to do what I enjoy with the writing, getting good feedback for the books that people enjoy and which can be seen to be making a positive difference.

Nick Sturgeon

Find Nick at www.nicksturgeonbooks.com

SIGN UP

9 781838 130435